Advance praise for

Walking Boston

"Walking Boston takes you to the heart of this great city. From historical Freedom Trail, to the beauty of Walden Woods, this one-of-a-kind book provides the most comprehensive walking guide for both tourists and long-time residents alike."

—Steve Upson, Publisher, *Boston Sports Journal*

"In the most walkable city you'll find, *Walking Boston* will be an indispensable guide to the can't-miss sites, eateries, and historic homes. . . ."

—Doug Most, Senior Editor, *Boston Magazine*

Help Us Keep This Guide Up to Date

Every effort has been made by the author and editors to make this guide as accurate and useful as possible. However, many things can change after a guide is published—establishments close, streets are rerouted, buildings change, facilities come under new management, etc.

We would love to hear from you concerning your experiences with this guide and how you feel it could be improved and be kept up to date. While we may not be able to respond to all comments and suggestions, we'll take them to heart and we'll also make certain to share them with the author. Please send your comments and suggestions to the following address:

The Globe Pequot Press
Reader Response/Editorial Department
P.O. Box 480
Guilford, CT 06437

Or you may e-mail us at:

editorial@globe-pequot.com

Thanks for your input, and happy travels!

Walking Boston

Greg Letterman and Katherine Hawkins Letterman

 Endorsed by the American Volkssport Association

FALCON®

GUILFORD, CONNECTICUT
An imprint of The Globe Pequot Press

> **To Elizabeth Stewart Clarke**
> A lady for whom Boston will always
> be a special place

_A_FALCONGUIDE®

Copyright © 2001 by The Globe Pequot Press

Falcon and FalconGuide are registered trademarks of The Globe Pequot Press.

Photo credits: Thanks to the National Parks Service, Massport, and Greg Letterman and Katherine Hawkins Letterman

Library of Congress Cataloging-in-Publication Data
Letterman, Greg.
    Walking Boston/Greg Letterman and Katherine Hawkins
    Letterman.—1st ed.
        p. cm.
    Includes bibliographical references and index.
    ISBN 1–56044–862–8
        1. Boston (Mass.)—Guidebooks. 2. Walking—Massachusetts—
Boston—Guidebooks. I. Letterman, Katherine Hawkins. II.Tittle.
III. Series.

F73.18.L48 2001
917.44'610444—dc21   2001023159

Manufactured in the United States of America
First Edition/First Printing

Contents

Acknowledgments

No book reaches the hands of readers without the critical efforts of many others in addition to those of its authors. Numerous people contributed to the creation of this book.

Our special thanks go to the Volkssport clubs of the Boston area, Two Town Walking Club and Walk'n Mass Volkssport Club—and particularly its members Charlie Smith, Betty Foley, Arlene Girouard, and Polly Meltzer.

We are also very appreciative of the staff of MassPort, particularly Georgeane Tacelli and Alice Gray; the staff of Garden in the Woods, particularly Barbara Pryor; enthusiastic East Boston citizens, particularly Edith Deangelis; the staff of the Boston Public Library; the staff of the Boston Athletic Association, particularly Jack Fleming; the staff of the Arnold Arboretum; the staff of the Peabody Essex Museum; and city, state, and federal park and tourism officials—all of whom were very helpful and supportive.

Ranne Warner suggested we include Garden in the Woods as one of our walks, resulting in obvious benefits for us and our readers.

Our gratitude goes, of course, to our initial editor, Judith Galas; our final editors, Gayle Shirley and Rick Newby; and to all the people at Falcon Publishing and the Globe Pequot Press who made the creation, publication, and distribution of this book possible.

Our daughters, Katie and Elizabeth Clarke, accompanied us on some of our walks and were always our great supporters.

Credit should be given also to those countless others who helped in ways big and small but who could not all be named here. And thanks, too, for you readers who have bought, used, and—we hope—benefited from and enjoyed this book.

Thank you all!

Foreword

For more than 20 years, Falcon has guided millions of people to America's wild outside, showing them where to paddle, hike, bike, bird, fish, climb, and drive. With this walking series, we at Falcon ask you to try something just as adventurous. We invite you to experience this country from its sidewalks, not its back roads, and to stroll through some of America's most interesting cities.

In their haste to get where they are going, travelers often bypass this country's cities, and in the process, they miss the historic and scenic treasures hidden among the bricks. Many people seek spectacular scenery and beautiful settings on top of the mountains, along the rivers, and in the woods. While nothing can replace the serenity and inspiration of America's natural wonders, we should not overlook the beauty of the urban landscape.

The steel and glass of municipal mountains reflect the sunlight and make people feel small in the shadows. Birds sing in city parks, water burbles in the fountains, and along the sidewalks walkers can still see abundant wildlife—their fellow human beings.

Falcon's many outdoor guidebooks have encouraged people not only to explore and enjoy America's natural beauty but to also preserve and protect it. Our cites are equally meant to be enjoyed and explored and their irreplaceable treasures need care and protection.

When travelers and walkers want to explore something that is inspirational and beautiful, we hope they will lace up their walking shoes and point their feet toward one of this country's many cities. For there, along the walkways, they are sure to discover the excitement, history, beauty, and charm of urban America.

—*The Editors*

Map Legend

Walk Route Direction   River or Stream

Interstate Highways   Lake or Pond

U.S. Highways   Boundary, State Park or Institution

State and County Roads   Fishing

Hiking/Walking Trail   Boat launch

Start/Finish of Loop Walk   Swimming

Parking Area   Railroad

Building   Map Orientation

Restrooms, Male and Female   Scale of Distance

Handicapped Access   Overlook or Point of Interest

Picnic Area

Playground

Overview Map–Greater Boston

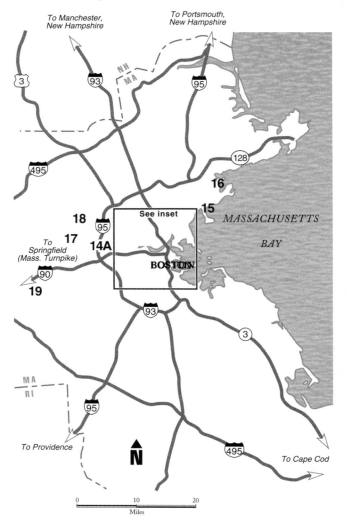

Inset Map–Municipal Boston

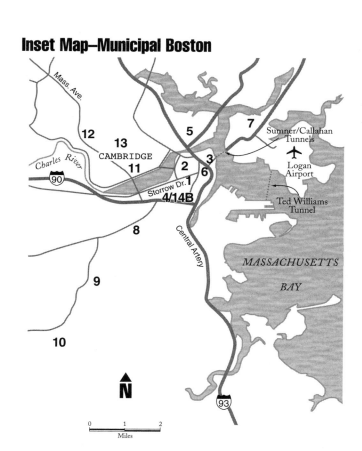

Preface: Come Walk Boston

Easily and enjoyably walkable, Boston is accessible to all. Wonderfully alive in every season and by both day and night, it does not try to be like any place else—and it is not. This book is written for the old resident, the new arrival, and the transient visitor (even those stranded at Logan Airport). Get to know Boston well. You will be glad you did. We fell in love with Boston. You will, too.

Boston is the site of early, important European settlement in America; the home of fishermen, sailors, and global traders; the scene of the starts of the Revolution, religious movements, and the abolitionism that led to the Civil War; a wealthy city with great buildings, public spaces, and institutions; the center of American literary, cultural, and intellectual life for over a century; a haven for many ethnic groups; and a place of natural (and cultivated) scenic beauties.

If you are only in Boston for a day, the Freedom Trail is a great walking option. Taking this book's Walks 1, 3, 5, and 6 will show you everything on that trail and much more.

This book takes you to places no other guidebook does, while assuring that you do not miss "must see" sights. It takes you from city center to neighborhoods and suburbs, along charming streets and among great architecture. Want to see a beach, Walden Pond, the Charles River, a Revolutionary War battlefield, Boston Harbor, Fenway Park, the Boston Marathon's "Heartbreak Hill," Cambridge, Salem, museums, universities, gardens, and historic districts? You will with this book—while getting good exercise; seeing fascinating, beautiful things; learning new, interesting facts about what you see; and gaining a real feel for the city!

the walks

Walk name	Difficulty	Distance (miles)	Time	♿	🏙	🌳	👪	🛍	🐕	📷
Boston's Core										
1. On and around the Common	Easy 1.5	2.00	1 hr	X		X	X		X	X
2. Beacon Hill and Black History Walk	Mixed 2.0	2.25	70 mns		X			X	X	X
3. North End	Easy 1.5	2.00	1 hr	X	X		X	X	X	X
4. Back Bay	Easy 1.0	2.25	70 mns	X	X		X	X	X	X
5. Waterfront	Easy 1.5	4.00*	2 hrs*		X		X			X
6. Downtown	Easy 1.0	2.00	1 hr	X	X		X	X	X	X
Peripheral City of Boston										
7. Logan Airport/East Boston	Easy 1.2	2.75	1.50 hr	X		X	X		X	X
8. The Fens	Easy 1.0	2.50	1.25 hr	X	X	X				X
9. Jamaica Pond and Victorian Jamaica Plain/Jamaica Plain	Easy 1.2	2.25	70 mns	X		X	X			X
10. Arnold Arboretum/Jamaica Plain	Easy 1.8	4.00	2 hrs	X	X	X	X			X

Boston's Inner Suburbs

				Wheelchair access	City setting	Nature setting	Good for kids	Shopping	Food	Bring camera
11. Along the Charles River/ Boston–Cambridge	Easy 1.5	3.75	1 hr 50 mns		X		X		X	X
12. Massachusetts Avenue/ Boston–Cambridge	Easy 1.5	3.00	1.5 hr		X		X	X	X	X
13. Cambridge	Easy 1.5	4.00	2 hrs		X		X	X	X	X
14. Boston Marathon:										
A) Heartbreak Hill/Newton	Moderate 3.0	5.00	2.5 hrs		X		X			X
B) Downtown/Back Bay, Boston	Easy 1.0	0.80	30 mns		X		X	X	X	X
15. Ocean Walk/Nahant-Lynn-Swampscott	Easy 1.0	2.00	1 hr			X	X		X	X

Boston's Outer Suburbs

				Wheelchair access	City setting	Nature setting	Good for kids	Shopping	Food	Bring camera
16. Salem	Easy 1.0	2.00	1 hr				X	X	X	X
17. Walden Pond/Concord-Lincoln	Easy 1.2	1.75	50 mns			X	X		X	X
18. Minute Man Trail/Lexington-Lincoln-Concord	Easy 1.8	5.00**	2.50 hrs**			X	X		X	X
19. Garden in the Woods/Framingham	Moderate 2.8	1.00	30 mns			X	X			X

* Unless using the MBTA ferry ** One way

the icons

Wheelchair access	City setting	Nature setting	Good for kids	Shopping	Food	Bring camera

Introduction

Walking the streets and boulevards of a city can take you into its heart and give you a feel for its pulse and personality. From the sidewalk looking up, you can appreciate its architecture. From the sidewalk peeking in, you can find the quaint shops, local museums, and great eateries that give a city its charm and personality. From a city's nature paths, you can smell the flowers, glimpse the wildlife, gaze at a lake, or hear a creek gurgle. Only by walking can you get close enough to read the historical plaques and watch the people. When you walk a city, you get it all—adventure, scenery, local color, good exercise, and fun.

Boston is safe and compact and can be easily walked by everyone. Extensive measures have been taken to make Boston accessible to the walking-impaired. Things of historical, architectural, natural, artistic, literary, and general interest may be seen—often all on the same walk. You need only look around you as you make your way.

Look above the ground floor from across the street or at a distance. Many buildings' ground floors were renovated for commercial uses but retained their charms or were further modified on their upper floors. You can see a building's beauty and read its history if you just look up. Read historical markers, statues' inscriptions, and other informative information along your walk. At public places, get free literature describing what you are seeing. Be guided but not restricted by a walk's route. If something off the route seems attractive, take a look. If an eye-catching thing is not described, look anyway. If a route is too long, walk a portion of it or cover part using public transportation. This book's walk routes do not cover everything of interest in Boston, in the areas of the walks, or even along the walk's routes.

How to use this guide

We have designed this book so that you can easily find the walks that match your interests, time, and energy level. The Trip Planner (see pages xiv–xv) is the first place you should look when deciding on a walk. This table will give you the basic information—a walk's distance, the estimated walking time, and difficulty. The pictures or icons in the table also tell you specific things about the walk:

Every walk has something of interest, but this icon tells you that the route will have particular appeal for the shutterbug. Be sure to bring your camera. You will have great scenic views or shots of interesting places and things.

Somewhere along the route you will have the chance to get food or a beverage. You will have to glance through the walk description to determine what kind of food and beverages are available and where. Walks that do not have the food icon probably are along nature trails or in noncommercial areas of the city.

During your walk you will have the chance to shop. More detailed descriptions of the types of stores you will find can be found in the actual walk description.

This walk features something kids will enjoy seeing or doing—a park, zoo, museum, or play equipment. In most cases the walks that carry this icon are short and follow an easy, fairly level path. You know your young walking companions best. If your children are patient walkers who do not tire easily, then feel free to choose walks that are longer and harder. In fact, depending on a child's age and energy, most children can do any of the walks in this book. The icon only notes those walks we think they will especially enjoy.

Your path will take you primarily through urban areas. Buildings, small city parks, and paved paths are what you will see and pass.

You will pass through a large park or walk in a natural setting where you can see and enjoy nature.

The wheelchair icon means that the path is fully accessible. This walk would be easy for someone pushing a wheelchair or stroller. We have made every attempt to follow a high standard for accessibility. The icon means there are curb cuts or ramps along the entire route, plus a wheelchair-accessible bathroom somewhere along the way. The path is mostly or entirely paved, and ramps and unpaved surfaces are clearly described. If you use a wheelchair and have the ability to negotiate curbs and dirt paths or to wheel for longer distances and on uneven surfaces, you may want to skim the directions for the walks that do not carry this symbol. You may find other walks you will enjoy. If in doubt, read the full text of the walk or call the contact source for guidance.

A note to joggers: Joggers also can enjoy many of the walks in this book. If you prefer to jog, first look for those walks with a rating of 1 or 2. These walks most likely are flat and have a paved or smooth surface. If you want something more challenging, read the walk descriptions to see if any harder routes appeal to you.

At the start of each walk description, you will find specific information describing the route and what you can expect on your walk:

General location: Here you will get the walk's general location in the city or within a specific area.

Special attractions: Look here to find the specific things you will pass. If this walk has museums, historic homes, restaurants, or wildlife, it will be noted here.

3

Difficulty rating: We have designed or selected walking routes that an ordinary person in reasonable health can complete. The walks are rated from 1 to 3, 1 being the easiest.

How easy or hard a walk may be depends on each person. But here are some general guidelines of what the number rating indicates:

A walk rated as Easy/1 is flat, with few or no hills. Most likely you will be walking on a maintained surface made of concrete, asphalt, wood, or packed earth. The path will be easy to follow, and you will be only a block or so from a phone, other people, or businesses. If the walk is less than a mile, you may be able to walk comfortably in street shoes.

Walks rated Moderate/2 may be partially on unpaved surfaces, be somewhat lengthy, and include some hills and crowded urban streets.

A walk rated as Difficult/3 could be longer and include more or steeper hills. Portions of the path may be stretches of sand, dirt, gravel, or small crushed rock. The single walk with this rating in *Walking Boston* is lengthy, mostly on pavement but with some poor gravel path portions, and along hilly suburban streets. You should wear walking shoes.

Walks falling between two of the above standard ratings have intermediate characteristics. If you are in doubt, read the walk text carefully or call the listed contact for more information.

Distance and estimated time: This gives the total distance of the walk. The time allotted for each walk is based on walking time only, which we have calculated at about 30 minutes per mile, a slow pace. Most people have no trouble walking a mile in half an hour, and people with some walking experience often walk a 20-minute mile. If the walk includes museums, shops, or restaurants, you may want to add sightseeing time to the estimate.

Services: Here you will find out if such things as restrooms, parking, refreshments, or information centers are available and where you are likely to find them.

Restrictions: The most often noted restriction is pets, which almost always have to be leashed in a city. Most cities also have strict "pooper-scooper" laws, and they enforce them. But restrictions may also include the hours or days a museum or business is open, age requirements, or whether you can ride a bike on the path. If there is something you cannot do on this walk, it will be noted here.

For more information: Each walk includes at least one contact source for you to call for more information. If an agency or business is named as a contact, you will find its phone number and address in Appendix B. This appendix also includes contact information for any business or agency mentioned anywhere in the book.

Getting started: Here you will find specific directions to the starting point. Most walks are closed loops, which means they begin and end at the same point. Thus, you do not have to worry about finding your car or your way back to the bus stop when your walk is over. Boston has great public transportation, so it may be easier—and sometimes even more interesting—to end a few of your walks away from the starting point. When this happens, you will get clear directions on how to take public transportation back to your starting point. If a walk is not a closed loop, this section will tell you where the walk ends, and you will find the exact directions back to your starting point at the end of the walk's directions. For any circular loop and for many other walks, it is possible to pick up a walk and end it at any point along its route.

Public transportation: Many cities have excellent transportation systems; others have limited services. If it is possible to take a bus or commuter train to the walk's starting point, you will find the bus or train noted here. You may also find some information about where the bus or train stops.

Overview: Every part of a city has a story. Here is where you will find the story or stories about the people, neighborhoods, and history connected to your walk.

The Walk

When you reach this point, you are ready to start walking. In this section you will find not only specific and detailed directions, but you will also learn more about the things you are passing. Those who want only the directions and none of the extras can find the straightforward directions by looking for the ➤.

What to wear

The best advice is to wear something comfortable. Leave behind anything that binds, pinches, rides up, falls down, slips off the shoulder, or comes undone. Otherwise, let common sense, the weather, and your own body tell you what to wear.

Your feet take the hardest pounding when you walk, so wear good shoes. Sandals, shoes with noticeable heels, or any shoe you rarely wear are not good choices. Some running shoes make superb walking shoes. Choose running shoes with wide heels, little or no narrowing under the arch, noticeable tread designs, and firm insoles.

If you will be walking in the sun, in the heat of the day, in the wind, or along a route with little or no shade, take along a hat or scarf and perhaps sunglasses.

A fanny pack comes in handy for holding water, keys, money, and sunglasses and leaves your hands free to read your directions. If walking several hours where there are few or no services, a light backpack will carry beverages and snacks.

What to take

Carry water even if you will be walking where refreshments are available. Strap a bottle to your fanny pack or tuck a small bottle in a pocket. Several small sips taken throughout a walk are more effective than one large drink at the walk's end. Avoid drinks with caffeine or alcohol. They deplete rather than replenish your body's fluids. If walking several miles with a dog, remember to take a small bowl so your pet can have a drink.

Sunscreen is important year-round. Take insect repellent if it may be needed.

Safety and street savvy

Mention a big city and many people immediately think of safety. Some questions are frequently asked: Is it safe to walk during the day? What about walking at night? What areas should I avoid?

You should use common sense whether you are walking in a small town or a big city, but safety does not have to be your overriding concern. American cities are enjoyable places, and if you follow some basic tips, you will find that they are generally safe places.

Any safety mishap in a large city is likely to come from petty theft or vandalism. So, the biggest tip is simple: Do not tempt thieves. Purses dangling on shoulder straps or slung over your arms, wallets peeking out of pockets, arms burdened with packages, valuables on the car seat—all of these things attract the pickpocket, purse snatcher, or thief. If you look like you could easily be relieved of your possessions, you may be.

Do not carry a purse. Put your money in a money belt or tuck your wallet into a deep side pocket of your pants or skirt or in a fanny pack that rides over your hip or stomach. Lock your valuables in the trunk of your car before you park and leave for your walk. Protect your camera by wearing the strap across your chest, not just over your shoulder. Better yet, put your camera in a backpack.

You also will feel safer if you remember the following:

- Be aware of your surroundings and the people near you.

- Avoid parks or other isolated places at night.

- Walk with others.

- Walk in well-lit and well-traveled areas.

The walks in this book were selected by people who had safety in mind. No walk will take you through a bad neighborhood or into an area of the city that is known to be dangerous. So relax and enjoy your walk.

Share the fun

We have tried to walk you to and through the best this city has to offer. But you surely will discover other wonderful things. Be sure to write us to share your discovery or interesting fact or to correct any errors. We would love to hear from you.

Meet Greater Boston

General

Counties: Suffolk, Essex, Middlesex, Norfolk, and Plymouth

Time zone: Eastern

Area codes: 508 (Framingham and Plymouth); 617 (Boston, Brookline, Cambridge, and Newton); 781 (Lexington, Lynn, Marblehead, and Wellesley); and 978 (Concord, Lowell, Salem, and Sudbury)

Size

640,700 people within city limits

4.4 million people in metro area

11.5 million visitors annually

59 square miles (3,000 square miles in metro area)

Elevation

Sea level to 235 feet above sea level

Climate

Average yearly precipitation: 43.43 inches

Average yearly humidity: 67 percent

Average yearly days of sunshine: 99

Average yearly snowfall: 42 inches

Average maximum temperature: 59 degrees F

Average minimum temperature: 44 degrees F

Getting there

Major highways

Interstates: I-90 (Massachusetts Turnpike, toll); I-93; I-95; and I-495

U.S. highways: 1 and 3

State highways: 1A, 2, 2A, 3, 9, 16, 28, 30, 107, and 128

Drives and Expressways: Storrow Memorial Drive; Memorial Drive; and Central Artery (Fitzgerald Expressway)

The Boston accent, made famous by President Kennedy, exists in variant forms all along the social totem pole.

Some distinctive pronunciations are of strictly Boston terms. "Quincy" is pronounced "Kwinzy"; "Peabody" like "PEE-buddy," with the last syllable unstressed and swallowed; "Concord" like "conquered"; Harvard's "Coop"—for "Cooperative"—sounds like a chicken "coop" and not a co-op.

"Faneuil," as in the hall and its donor, was originally pronounced "Funnel," although today most Bostonians pronounce it "Fan-yule."

Some words are unique to Boston or its region. "Wicked good" is a positive superlative. The "T" in T Stop, a public relations invention, stands for nothing. When waiters and others say "scrod," they mean young cod, and if an "H" is used ("shcrod"), young haddock is the principal ingredient. Scrod is really an acronym of "Special Catch Received on Dock" and is the cheapest white-fleshed fish then available.

"Frappes" (pronounced "fraps") are what most Americans call milk shakes. In Boston, a "milk shake" contains no ice cream at all and is merely milk mixed with flavorings. "Jimmys" are sprinkles for topping ice cream cones. A "tonic" is New England's term for a soft drink.

Now if asked if you speak "Boston," you may say with assurance "Shoe-ah" (sure).

Bridges and tunnels: Charlestown Bridge; Charles River Dam; Harvard Bridge; Tobin Bridge (toll); Callahan/Sumner Tunnels (toll); and Ted Williams Tunnel (toll)

Airport service (Logan International, Boston, "L"; Manchester, NH, "M"; T. F. Green International, Providence, RI, "G"; and Bradley Field, Hartford, CT/Springfield, MA, "B")

Aer Lingus (L), Air Alliance (B), Air Canada (L), Air France (L), Air Nova (L), Air Ontario (G, B), Air Tran (L), Alitalia (L), America West (L, B), American (L, G, B), American Eagle (L, M, G, B), American Trans Air (L), ASA Delta Connection (M), British Airways (L), Business Express (L, G), Cape Air (L, G), Comair (L, M, B), Continental (L, M, G, B), Continental Express (M, B), Delta Air Lines (L, G, B), Delta Express (L, G, B), Frontier (L), Icelandair (L), KLM (L), Korean Air (L), Lufthansa (L), MetroJet (L, M, B), Midway (L, B), Midwest Express (L, B), Northwest Airlines (L, M, G, B), Olympic (L), Qantas (L), Sabena (L), Shuttle America (B), Southwest Airlines (M, G, B), Sun Country (L), Swissair (L), TAP Air Portugal (L), TWA (B), TWA Express (B), United (L, M, G, B), United Express (L), US Airways (L, M, G, B), US Airways Express (L, M, G, B), US Airways Shuttle (L), and Virgin Atlantic (L)

Rail service
Amtrak
Massachusetts Bay Transportation Authority (MBTA) commuter rail service—sometimes referred to as the "Purple Line"
MBTA "T" subway/elevated rail/trolley

Bus service
Bonanza Bus Lines
Greyhound
LIFT (Local Intra-Framingham Transit) within Framingham
MBTA buses

Peter Pan Trailways
Plymouth & Brockton Street Railway Company
Salem Trolley (within central Salem)

Water transportation
A.C. Cruise Line
Airport Water Shuttle
Bay State Cruise Company
Boston Harbor Cruises
City Water Taxi
Harbor Express
Massachusetts Bay Lines
MBTA Inner Harbor Ferry Service

Recreation

Boston has it all—high culture, professional athletics, numerous sports facilities of every sort, the nearby ocean, and the variety that comes from being the ultimate college town.

Major industries

Boston's many institutions of higher learning and their students provide the city with a distinctive flavor. Boston has long been a major financial and insurance center. It has recently developed an extensive high-technology base and become a major tourism destination point.

Media

Television stations
WBZ (CBS)—Channel 4
WCVB (ABC)—Channel 5
WFXT (FOX)—Channel 25
WGBH (PBS)—Channel 2
WGBX (PBS) – Channel 44
WHDH (NBC)—Channel 7
WLVI (WBN)—Channel 56

Radio stations
WBCN 104.1 FM—Alternative
WBMX 98.5 FM—Hot adult contemporary
WBOS 92.9 FM—Adult rock
WBUR 90.9 FM—News/talk
WBZ 1030 AM—News/talk
WCRB 102.5 FM—Classical
WEEI 850 AM—Sports
WEGQ 93.7 FM—Oldies
WGBH 89.7 FM—Classical
WHRB 95.3 FM—Classics/jazz
WILD 1090 AM—Urban
WJMN 94.5 FM—Contemporary hits
WKLB 99.5 FM—Country
WMJX 106.7 FM—Adult contemporary
WODS 103.3 FM—Oldies
WRKO 680 AM—News/talk
WROR 105.7 FM—Adult contemporary
WTKK 96.9 FM—Smooth jazz
WXKS 1430 AM—Oldies
WXKS 107.9 FM—Contemporary hits
WZLX 100.7 FM—Classic rock

Newspapers/magazines
Boston Globe
Boston Herald
Boston Magazine

Special annual events

- January: Boston Cooks Kitchen/Culinary Expo
- February: New England Boat Show
- March: Evacuation Day/St. Patrick's Day; New England Spring Flower Show
- April: Patriot's Day/Boston Marathon; Freedom

Trail Week; Placing the Lanterns in Old North Church, North End

- May: Ducklings Day Parade; Street Performers Festival, Faneuil Hall Marketplace; Lilac Sunday, Arnold Arboretum; Hidden Gardens of Beacon Hill Tour

- June: Ancient and Honorable Artillery Company Parade, Boston Common; Bunker Hill Day Parade, Charlestown; Rose Garden Party, Back Bay Fens; Salem Maritime Festival; Longfellow House Festival of Music and Poetry; North End Italian Festivals; Boston Pops Free Concerts, Hatch Shell; Harborlights concerts

- July: Reading of the Declaration of Independence from the Old State House; Boston Pops Fourth of July Concert/Fireworks, Hatch Shell; Boston Seaport Festival; North End Italian Festivals; Boston Pops Free Concerts, Hatch Shell; Harborlights concerts

- August: Shakespeare in the Park, Boston Common; North End Italian Festivals; Boston Pops Free Concerts, Hatch Shell; Harborlights concerts

- September: Cambridge River Festival; Essex Institute Harvest Festival, Salem

- October: Head of the Charles Regatta (crew rowing competition); Haunted Happenings, Salem

- November: Holiday Arts Celebration, Faneuil Hall; Boston Annual Antiquarian Book Fair; Thanksgiving Dinner, Plymouth

- December: First Night celebrations, Central Boston; Reenactment of the Boston Tea Party

Weather

Boston has a moderate climate with four distinct seasons. No special walking precautions are necessary due to weather, if you dress appropriately for the day. Although the ocean moderates extreme temperatures, you will be able to do things in one season that are unavailable in another. Boston is comfortably walkable in any season, but winter generally holds the least charms. Some outdoor venues close in winter. November and December are the wettest months. Winters average about 31 degrees F. Springs and—particularly—autumns are usually glorious. Autumn temperatures range from 50 to 70 degrees F. Summers sometimes reach 90 with lows in the 60s.

The U.S. Meteorological Service says Boston is the windiest U.S. city. Storms called "Nor'easters" (which blow in from the northeast) are a real threat. In April 1997, the day after Bostonians sunned in their gardens, a Nor'easter dropped 18 inches of snow. Nor'easter winds and waves wreak havoc.

By degrees Fahrenheit and inches of precipitation, Boston's average daily temperature (high/low) ranges and total precipitation (rain/snow) by month are: January: 36/21—4/12; February: 38/23—3.7/11; March: 46/30—4.1/7; April: 57/40—3.7/1; May: 67/50—3.5/0; June: 77/59—2.9/0; July: 82/65—2.7/0; August: 80/63—3.7/0; September: 71/58—3.4/0; October: 62/48—3.4/0; November: 51/39—4.2/2; and December: 40/27—4.5/7.

Transportation

By car: The first and best rule for driving in the center of Boston is "Do not!" The streets are a labyrinth and often narrow and crowded. They usually run one way and not the way you want to go. Boston drivers are universally recognized as among the world's worst. Public parking spaces are few, often restricted to neighborhood residents, and

The Big Dig

The Third Harbor/Central Artery Project, known as the "Big Dig," was begun in 1990 and is now in full swing. The Big Dig will take the elevated Central Artery, the main north-south freeway going through Central Boston (which divided neighborhoods and is unsightly) and put it underground and out of sight—replacing it with a 100-acre green park. The project will cost at least $20.4 billion—the most expensive U.S. highway project ever—and will not be completed until 2005 (or even 2010!). Work on it will block roads and disrupt traffic and pedestrian routes and may invalidate some route instructions in this book (particularly Walks 3 and 6) as work progresses. While this is taking place, you may contact "SmartRoutes," (617) 374-1234, to locate problem areas and means of circumventing them. Stay informed!

subject to complex and restrictive rules. Commercial parking is available but expensive and sometimes full. A common Boston crime is breaking into parked cars in heavily touristed areas.

If you want to go by car, take a taxi. They are plentiful, may be called by telephone for pick-up service, or may be hailed on the street. Public transportation in the center of Boston is readily available, quick, and relatively inexpensive. Take public transportation into and around the center of Boston and leave your car somewhere safe and off the street at some point on the T line from which your walk begins or ends and distant from Boston's center. There are commercial parking lots adjacent to a number of T stops. For the Red Line, try those adjacent to Alewife T to the north and Braintree T to the south. For the Green Line, try the lot next to Riverside T Stop. For the Orange Line, try those adjacent to Forest Hills T to the south and Sullivan Square T to the north. For the Blue Line, try the lots adjacent to the Orient Heights and Wonderland T stops.

When taking walks outside Boston's center, it will often be much more convenient to take a private vehicle than to use public transportation (but never forget—many of the drivers on the road with you are Bostonians!). Nonetheless, each walk in this book may be made using public transportation.

Boston streets rarely follow a grid pattern. Boston has short streets, crooked streets, and streets that are actually only tunnels or stairs. Boston's politicians name everything possible for some political constituent, seemingly calling every street corner a "square" after someone few ever heard of. Street names change frequently along their routes. Every map will give conflicting information on their names, their locations, and where the name change occurs. Boston has many charms. Coherency in the way its streets are laid out, named, and marked is not one.

When driving, be advised that Boston, and New England generally, give signage for the streets you are crossing and not for the major street you are on. In general, informative signage along the roads of outer metropolitan Boston will be less than thorough and clear. Multi-street intersections in Boston are frequently managed by traffic circles/rotaries/roundabouts. When entering a rotary, remember that cars already in the rotary have the right of way. Unless otherwise marked, speed limits in town are 30 miles per hour. Right turns on red are permitted after a full stop.

Getting to Boston by automobile is easy (in the sense that the major highways will take you there), if sometimes confusing. Two major circumferential highways largely circle Boston. The nearer is *Massachusetts Route 128,* which lies in a radius about 10 miles from Boston's center. The farther is *U.S. Interstate Highway 495,* which lies in a radius of about 20 miles.

U.S. Interstate Highway 90 (the Massachusetts Turnpike) is a toll road running east and west into and out of Boston. It intersects with I-93/Central Artery.

U.S. Interstate Highway 95 is a north-south highway coming north into Boston from Providence, Rhode Island, and going north from Boston toward coastal Maine. It really neither enters nor leaves Boston since politics and local opposition prevented its continuation through Boston itself. Parts of the existing Route 128 were designated I-95 to fill the gap between the northern and southern parts of the "real" I-95. No one in Boston calls this I-95. It is invariably orally referred to as Route 128.

U.S. Interstate Highway 93 is a north-south highway that comes south from New Hampshire, enters Boston as the Central Artery (which provides continuity for this route), and joins I-95 for a while before disappearing from maps as a numbered highway. At points, I-95 south is also I-93 north. Boston is that kind of place.

The *Central Artery (Fitzgerald Expressway)* is the freeway running north-south through Central Boston and connecting the northern and southern parts of I-93. *Storrow Memorial Drive* runs west on the Boston side of the Charles River from Charles River Dam. *Memorial Drive* parallels Storrow Drive on the Cambridge side of the river.

As you approach Boston, you will discover that it is often difficult to make the trip into the city's center because the water surrounding Boston necessitates entry and exit through a number of bottleneck tunnels and bridges.

Become familiar with the major bridges and tunnels that provide access to Central Boston. Ted Williams Tunnel and Sumner/Callahan Tunnels connect Central Boston with East Boston/Logan Airport. Charlestown Bridge crosses the Charles River between the North End and Charlestown. Tobin Bridge crosses the Mystic River between Charlestown and Chelsea. Harvard Bridge and Charles River Dam are principal among the bridges that cross the Charles River from Boston to Cambridge.

By air: More than 40 airlines serve Boston via Logan International Airport, just 2 miles from downtown Boston. Getting to and from Logan by car or public transport is relatively easy. Some choose—for convenience of location, availability of flights, or cost—to get to Boston by flying into and out of airports in Providence, Rhode Island or Manchester, New Hampshire. Others prefer Bradley Field serving Hartford, Connecticut/Springfield, Massachusetts.

By train: Amtrak operates from South Station at Summer Street and Atlantic Avenue via Back Bay Station at 145 Dartmouth Street.

MBTA runs 13 commuter rail service lines, sometimes referred to as the "Purple Line," extending as far as 60 miles from Boston. The Purple Line runs from South Station as far as Worcester; Needham Heights; Forge Park; Providence, Rhode Island; Stoughton; Middleboro; Kingston; and Plymouth and from North Station at 159 Portland as far as Lowell, Fitchburg, Haverhill, Newburyport, and Rockport.

MBTA's "T" is a network of several lines—each designated by a color: Red, Orange, Green, or Blue—that operate as subways, elevated trains, and/or streetcars at various points along their routes. The T runs often and to most places you want to go (although routing between points involving different lines may be indirect and lengthy). System maps are available at many T stops and at other locations. Get one! The T stops running every night at 12:45 A.M. and does not begin again until 5 A.M.(6 A.M. on Sundays). Park Street Station and Downtown Crossing are the two "centers" for the T. Trains going to them are "inbound." Trains going from them are "outbound." Entrance to the T is by tokens sold at windows in most stations, with each ride—for however long and to whatever destination (except Green Line extensions for inbound service)—available at a single price. Special discounted "Visitor Passports" for unlimited use on the T and city buses for different lengths of time are also available.

By bus: For information about bus service in the greater Boston area, call MBTA. Fares are by exact change or token only. There are 170 bus routes. Bus service is good and convenient. It may provide a more direct connection than the T for some routes and will take you to and from many places not served by the T. LIFT operates within Framingham, and the Salem Trolley plies a tourist route within Salem.

Greyhound operates from South Station. All other bus lines operate from a common terminal near South Station at 555 Atlantic Avenue. Peter Pan Trailways services western Massachusetts, Connecticut, and New York. Plymouth & Brockton Street Railway Company runs to and from Cape Cod. Bonanza Bus Lines serves both Cape Cod and Providence, Rhode Island.

By water: One of the most charming things you can do in Boston is to take advantage of its location on Boston Harbor. One of the most unusual ways to do this is to utilize, where possible, water transportation in lieu of other ground transportation. The City Water Taxi runs from Logan Airport's Harbor Ferry Terminal to landings throughout Boston Harbor from 6 A.M.. to 8 P.M. daily from April through mid-October and is available for other special hires or trips in the Boston Harbor vicinity. Mass-Port's Airport Water Shuttle runs regular routes year-round between Boston's Rowes Wharf and Harbor Ferry Terminal, a 7-minute trip (and no traffic jams). Harbor Express operates the Salem Ferry (a modern, stylish, high-speed catamaran), which runs—during the months of July through October, twelve trips daily, seven days a week—a triangular route from Harbor Ferry Terminal to the Harbor Express Docking Terminal at Boston's Long Wharf and from there to the Salem Ferry Landing. Harbor Express runs a similar triangular service to Quincy Shipyard (25 minutes between Quincy and Long Wharf). Boston Harbor Cruises runs a triangular service between Long Wharf, Boston Harbor Islands, and Hingham as well as providing transportation between Long Wharf and Provincetown. A.C. Cruise Line runs a route from 290 Northern Avenue Pier to Salem and Gloucester. MBTA runs commuter boats between Hingham (Hewitt's Cove) and Rowes Wharf, as does Massachusetts Bay Lines, and between Hull and Long Wharf, as well as ferries to Charlestown Navy Yard from Long Wharf and from Lovejoy Wharf (South Station) and a ferry from Lovejoy Wharf to the Federal Courthouse and the World Trade Center. From the World Trade Center, Bay State Cruise Company operates a route to Provincetown. Before taking one of these ferries or taxis, call ahead to check if these services are still available or if others have been added.

Safety

Walking Boston presents few serious safety issues. Boston was listed as the nation's second safest walking city in 2000 by the Surface Transportation Policy Project. No walk in this book will take you into an inherently dangerous neighborhood. Boston's climate and topography do not cause safety concerns. Nonetheless, bad things can happen to anyone anywhere. Be cautious. Be wise. Crowds are usually safer than empty streets. The day offers lesser perils than the night. Parts of Boston have unsavory reputations. These are best avoided.

Pickpockets and persons breaking into parked automobiles are common throughout the Boston area at places of high tourist concentrations.

Bostonians are incorrigible jaywalkers. But don't you do it! It is against the law. Be sensible. Cross wherever possible at protected crossings using zebra stripes, stop signs, or stoplights. Press buttons provided at crosswalks in order to obtain a protected crossing.

The biggest danger in Boston is driving on the streets and roads with local drivers. This peril cannot be overstressed. Bostonians may survive under these conditions, but you as a stranger may not and you will certainly not enjoy it. Avoid driving in Boston if you can!

The Story of Boston

Boston is wonderfully unique. Bostonians are inordinately proud of their city. What other city calls itself "The Hub of the Universe?" A brief recitation of its history will show you why.

Others lived in the Boston area before the Puritans came. Because Boston's future center was too harsh for permanent habitation, the Massachusetts and Wampanoag tribes' nearest settlements were in Jamaica Plain. The original Massachusetts Bay Colony seal—a grass-skirted native with the Latin inscription, "Come Over and Help Us"—proved inapt. During or following the 1675 King Philip's War, white settlers killed or exiled almost all local natives. Captain John Smith sailed up and named the Charles River in 1614. Pilgrims came to the area by 1620. William Blackstone, a chaplain for a failed 1623 English settlement, remained behind in isolation when his fellow settlers returned to their homeland. When Puritans had to leave Charlestown because of drought, he invited them to join him in what was to be Boston. They did, confiscated his land, and "gave" him back about 50 acres—now the Common. He left in anger. The dissolute English lawyer Thomas Morton's Merry Mount encampment at Quincy irritated Puritans until they drove him away.

Boston's Puritans—different from Pilgrims—came from England, many from Boston, Lancashire (originally St. Botolph's), in 1630 for religious reasons. Prosperous, conservative, and well educated, they wanted to "purify" Anglicanism of Roman Catholic practices. Puritans came not to establish freedom of religion but to practice *their* religion. Their theocracy's ministers were both political and moral leaders and expelled or persecuted many non-Puritans. Puritans created institutions that survive and put an imprint on Boston's character that persists.

The land they came to was first called Shawmut—Algonquin meaning "place of flowing waters"—Peninsula. Europeans also named it Trimountain or Tremont for its three peaks. Boston lay between the tidal Charles River and Boston Harbor, attached to the mainland by a neck so narrow that ships docked on either side obstructed traffic with their bowsprits. Its soil was infertile. It was too mountainous to live on or farm. To make the land more habitable, Puritans filled in smaller ponds and coves. Boston's topography's first big change came in 1811 when Beacon Hill's top 60 feet were removed. Landfill joined East Boston's five islands into one about 1830, and Bostonians filled in Back Bay over a 30-year period after 1857. These changes made Boston's modern core about four times larger than when the Puritans arrived. The process continues.

Devastating fires, one in 1676, another in 1711, and a third in 1760, cumulatively burned most of Boston. A fourth in 1872 leveled 65 acres and 776 buildings in the commercial district's center. The Revolution resulted in much damage. A 1919 North End flood—of molasses—killed 21. Some argue that urban renewal has been another disaster.

Bostonians prospered from the sea and their drive and ingenuity. Cod exports created a "cod aristocracy." Massachusetts exploited its forests and the "triangular trade" where African slaves were traded for Caribbean sugar that was made into rum that was then traded for more slaves. It benefited from nonenforcement of British legislation forbidding American manufacturing and maritime trade. With enforcement, Boston held a "Tea Party." Britain closed Boston's port in retaliation, depopulating and impoverishing Boston until 1805. The Napoleonic Wars gave New England merchants global commercial maritime primacy, since only belligerents' ships were subject to enemy attack. The War of 1812 again devastatingly closed Boston's port. Deprived by war of British goods, New Englanders manufactured their own. With peace, their goods sold around the world—many carried on Boston's ships. Boston traded with Asia in the clipper ships it made. It transported miners to California and brought their gold home. Boston marketed much of the world's wool. Boston dealt in anything, anywhere, and with anybody. When railroads and canals were built, Boston's financiers and insurance companies served the market and made their fortunes. Boston's thinkers and authors created an industry—publishing—that for decades was nationally dominant. Education, with 50 institutions of higher learning, is big business. Twentieth-century politics and a changed economy and technology left Boston in decline. Only since the late 1970s has Boston known economic renewal from high technology industries fostered by local universities.

Boston's resistance to British economic interference led to the Revolutionary War. Bostonians were the leaders in creating American support for armed revolt against British colonial rule. Boston's opposition to British measures resulted in the closing of its harbor, its military occupation, and the Redcoats' march on Concord. Pitched battles in and near Boston demonstrated American resolve and the Patriots' fighting ability. With the start of the Revolution, occupied Boston was besieged by George Washington's American troops. American cannons on Dorchester Heights left Boston and Boston Harbor at the Americans' mercy. The British negotiated withdrawal.

Once the British and their Tory supporters left on March 17, 1776, Boston no longer played a direct part during the rest of the war.

Religion and religious ministers were important to Boston. Congregationalism began with the Puritans' 1630 Convention Covenants. Puritan John Cotton was the first of Boston's powerful religious leaders. He was succeeded by the Mather dynasty. Roger Williams, America's first Baptist leader and founder of Rhode Island, was driven from Boston in 1635. Famed revivalist George Whitefield came in 1740. His Boston and Cambridge meetings drew thousands. His preaching was considered quite powerful. John Cheverus was beloved by Bostonians. People of all sects contributed to building his cathedral in 1803, rejoiced when he became Boston's first Roman Catholic bishop in 1810, and took pride when he was made a cardinal in 1836. Modern American Unitarianism, which merged with Universalism in 1961 with world headquarters in Boston, dates from 1825 and developed here. Transcendentalism, a religio-philosophical, latter-nineteenth-century movement, began among Boston-area intellectuals. William Miller drove Boston into a frenzy in 1843. Drawing on the Book of Revelations, Miller calculated the date of the end of the world—April 23, 1843. The faithful shut their shops, gave away their possessions, and waited. Nothing happened! Although Miller set a new date, few believed him. His reinterpreted tenets are the basis for modern-day Adventist sects. Mary Baker Eddy formulated Christian Science in the Boston area, and the sect's world headquarters is here today.

Boston is known for its class and ethnic divisions. Boston's mid-nineteenth-century established families were called "Brahmins." The term either derives from

India's priestly high caste or from the American premiere in Boston of Johannes Brahms's Second Symphony, considered outrageous at the time. Although some prominent Bostonians stayed until the performance's end, others left in indignation. Brahmins took themselves seriously as a class, exercised local power in community life, operated under their own social standards and customs, and generally exclusively intermarried and socialized. They were often not descendants of earlier Puritan notables—mostly Tories who left America after the Revolution—but the offspring of country lads who prospered by filling the vacuum left by departed Tories. Two prominent Brahmin families gave rise to John Collins Bossidy's 1910 toast, "And this is good old Boston, the home of the bean and the cod, Where the Lowells talk to Cabots, and the Cabots talk only to God." Brahmins are still around, but as a class they are largely powerless.

The Irish challenged early settlers' dominance. From a flow in the 1830s, Irish immigration became a flood with the failures of Irish potato harvests and resultant famine during the latter 1840s. Irish came to Boston, closer to Europe than other U.S. ports, because fares were cheap. Their arrival forever changed Boston. Irishmen fled a calamity; a country governed as a colony with alien—and alienated—landlords; a place losing its language but uncomfortable with English; and a squalid, dispirited society. They arrived hungry, and resented. "Bostonians" resented and feared the Irish but wanted strong Irish backs at cheap wages for hard labor. They took personal and legal measures to exclude Irishmen from private and public opportunities. Irishmen did not like that. They became American patriots but never forgot their common Irish blood. They gained political power and assured they would not lose it. The Irish remain prominent in Boston politics.

Boston dominated America in education, literature, and publishing for almost a century. Harvard University and Massachusetts Institute of Technology are, perhaps, the best-known local educational institutions. Ralph Waldo Emerson, Nathaniel Hawthorne, Henry David Thoreau, Henry James, and Henry Wadsworth Longfellow are just a few of the literary names associated with Boston. Boston still leads the nation in university education and in many intellectual advances.

Frugal and unostentatious, Bostonians appreciate beauty and grandeur and are willing to spend to get (and preserve) it. The handsome old and new architecture, the gardens, the museums, the public art, and the air of restrained, somewhat antique elegance that permeates the city are proof. Marvelous architects and designers such as Charles Bulfinch, Henry Hobson Richardson, Ogden Codman, Jr., and Frederick Law Olmsted helped make the Boston we know.

Today's Boston is an amalgam of much history; many ethnicities, religions, and social classes; great variety in architectural styles and cultural tastes; and individual idiosyncrasies in a beautiful natural setting. Boston and Bostonians are truly unique!

Walk 1

On and around the Common

General location: Central Boston.

Special attractions: The Common, the Public Garden, Park Street Church, the Granary Burying Ground, the *Cheers* bar, and many other architectural and historic sites.

Difficulty rating: Easy; gentle slope over pavement and protected crossings.

Distance: 2 miles.

Estimated time: 1 hour.

Services: Restrooms and water are available at the Common Visitor Information Center and the Frog Pond. Food and drink are available throughout.

On and around the Common

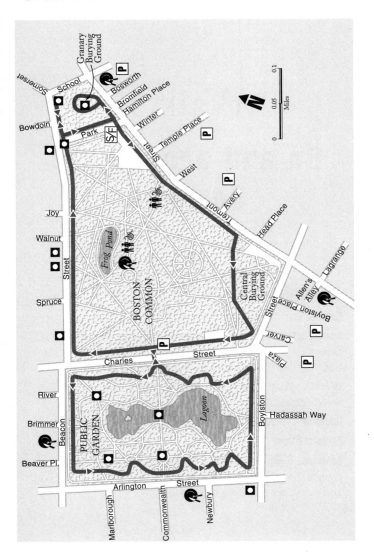

Restrictions: None. Possible difficulties for walking-impaired at Granary Burying Ground. At the Common/Public Garden, no skateboarding, rollerblading, or bicycling. Dogs must be leashed and their droppings retrieved. In the Public Garden, do not play games on the grass, walk on tree roots, pick flowers, or climb trees. Littering, as well as loitering after 10 P.M., are prohibited there. Gravestone rubbing is banned at any Boston-maintained historical cemetery.

For more information: Contact the Common Visitor Information Center.

Getting started: Start at Park Street T Stop's exit on the Common near Park and Tremont Streets. Drivers access this walk from the north, south, and west by exit 26 off I-93/Central Artery to Charles Street. Stay on Charles Street for 0.7 mile (keeping to the route prescribed below to avoid one-way problems on Charles). At Beacon, turn left and take the first available right onto Park to near the corner with Tremont, where you will see the Park Street T Stop. To reach covered commercial parking (wheelchair accessible, 6.25 feet clearance) under the Common, circle the Common—turning right on Tremont, right on Boylston, and then right on Charles—and enter the lot as marked from Charles's right lane. After exiting the garage, walk diagonally due east across the Common to the start point.

Public transportation: Red and Green T Lines stop at the Park Street Stop. MBTA bus routes 55 and 43 stop at Park and Tremont immediately adjacent to the readily visible start point.

Overview: This is the essential "getting-to-know-the-real-Boston" walk. Much of what Boston is famous for and what you came to see can be found along this walk—history, architecture, nature, human and literary interest stories, and people watching—plus it is an excellent way to stretch your legs in the middle of a great city.

The Common is America's first public park, the site of many important and interesting historical events, and the location of the *Shaw Memorial* and other statuary. The Public Garden, a place of great beauty, is America's first public botanical garden. A distinction is made between the Common—owned by all, with libertarian rules of conduct—and the Public Garden—"publicly owned," with restrictive rules.

Across Beacon Street from the Common are the State House—Massachusetts's elegant capitol—and some of the finest homes and clubs of Beacon Hill's elite Brahmins. Across Beacon from the Public Garden is TV's *Cheers* bar. Also included on this walk are visits to the Athenaeum, an old and famed private library; Park Street Church, the scene of many important "firsts"; and the Granary Burying Ground, final resting place for many early famous Bostonians, including John Hancock (at least parts of him) and Benjamin Franklin's parents. You will see all this and more on this must-do walk. We recommend it be your first Boston adventure.

The Walk

►Start at Park Street T Stop's exit, turn right, and walk a few feet to near Tremont Street.

The 1897 Park Street station is an original part of the first U.S. subway system. Lilli Ann Rosenberg's 1978 mosaic mural, near the Green Level entrance, is where excavation began in 1895. Braces between the mosaic's panels are original tunnel supports.

Boston Common is America's oldest public park, created in 1634. No part may be sold or leased, nor may any building or road be built on it. Its 48 acres are bounded by Tremont, Boylston, Charles, Beacon, and Park Streets. Originally almost unwooded, it was common grazing land for Bostonians' dairy cows until 1830. It was the site of public meetings, hangings and other punishments, the training of troops and militia, burials, sports and games, and social strolls. Lafayette, George Washington, Reverend George Whitefield, Martin Luther King, Amelia Bloomer, and Pope John Paul II all spoke here. In 1775, about 1,750 British troops encamped here and entrenched and fortified it.

►Turn right near Tremont on the Common's perimeter path, before reaching the streetside sidewalk, with the Common on your right and Tremont on your left. Walk about a half mile to the iron fence around the Central Burying Ground.

Near the start on your right is a 1924 monument honoring Lafayette's 1824 Boston visit. Across Tremont just past Winter Street stands Alexander Parris's 1820 Cathedral Church of Saint Paul, Boston's Episcopalian cathedral.

As you proceed, next on your right—just beyond the 1960 Parkman Plaza—is the Visitor Information Center/Park Ranger Station.

Next on your left you will encounter the 1925 Declaration of Independence Plaque and 100 feet farther on, Robert Kraus's 1888 *Boston Massacre Memorial*. The bronze figure represents Revolution breaking the chains of Tyranny. The relief figures depict the Boston Massacre's events (see Walk 6). One figure is Crispus Attucks, the first slain. Shaking "his" extended hand is considered good luck, but that is *not* Attucks's hand. He lies in the foreground with a shoe toe shiny from hopeful touches.

➤When you see, to your right, the 1756 Central Burying Ground—part of the Common since 1839—leave the perimeter path for the interior path that passes immediately right of the cast-iron fence enclosing the cemetery. Follow the fence 0.15 mile to Boylston Street near its intersection with Charles.

The Burying Ground's most famous occupants lie in unmarked graves—the composer William Billings and the painter Gilbert Stuart, whose portrait of George Washington is on the dollar bill. Here in a mass grave are the bones of approximately 1,000 people unearthed during subway construction.

➤Near Boylston, turn right, rejoining the perimeter path, with the Common on your right and Boylston and then Charles on your left, for about 0.1 mile. Walk to the designated Charles crosswalk.

The other side of Boylston, between Tremont and Charles, is known as "Piano Row." During the nineteenth and early twentieth centuries, this was Boston's and America's center for piano building and music publishing.

On Boylston just past Tremont is the 1889 Colonial Theatre—Boston's oldest theater surviving intact under its original name.

Charles Street was once almost all under water and gave the Common a shoreline at its lower end. Young Ben Franklin fished and played here. British troops left from here by ship for the battles that started the Revolution and reportedly buried here some of those battles' casualties. Near the crosswalk is the commemorative plaque for Pope John Paul II's 1979 papal mass.

➤Cross Charles at the crosswalk. Enter the Public Garden's gates, and stop.

The Public Garden is reclaimed land. Once part of Round Marsh that bordered the Common where Charles Street now lies, its 24 acres are bounded by Charles, Beacon, Arlington, and Boylston Streets. From its creation in 1838 it has been a public garden. America's first public botanical garden, it has 57 formal flowerbeds, more than 124 labeled specimen trees, and a variety of ornamental sculptures and fountains. The bridge over the lagoon was the world's shortest suspension bridge until reinforced with steel and concrete early in the twentieth century. There is much to see and enjoy. Explore the interior on your own.

Immediately to your right is Bela Pratt's 1923 statue of Reverend Everett Hale. Although U.S. Senate chaplain, he is best known for his short story, "Man Without a Country." Before you lie the Public Garden Lagoon, the Swan Boats, and the direct path to Arlington. The Swan Boat from Richard Wagner's opera *Lohengrin* inspired Boston's Swan Boats; they date from 1877. The Paget family has operated the Swan Boat concession since its creation. Originally the boats consisted of two joined canoes driven by a man pedaling a bicycle-like device turning paddleblades. On its stern, hiding the pedaler, was a representation of a large swan. The eight modern Swan Boats are much larger, each holding up to 20 passengers.

►Turn right on the interior perimeter path bordering the garden's cast-iron fence (remain on this path until you exit these same gates) and proceed about 0.1 mile to near Charles and Beacon.

Near Beacon, look left down the interior path to see Nancy Schön's 1987 cast bronze *Make Way for Ducklings* statues of Mrs. Mallard and her ducklings, from Robert

McCloskey's 1941 children's book of the same name. The largest is 40 inches high, and they stretch for 35 feet. A Giant Redwood tree stands 50 feet to their left.

➤Turn left on the path near Beacon's intersection and continue along Beacon about 0.1 mile to near Beacon and Arlington.

Across Beacon just before Beaver Place, note the *Cheers* bar—actually the Bull & Finch Pub—under the Hampshire House Restaurant. This 1909 Georgian Revival private residence was designed inside and out by Ogden Codman, Jr.

➤Near Arlington, turn left and stay on the path about 0.2 mile to near Arlington and Boylston.

Across Arlington, the buildings generally reflect 1850s French architectural styles—usually brownstone, mansard-roofed, freestanding groups of buildings designed to look like a single, grand building. The Mansard Block at the corner of Arlington and Beacon is an example.

Ahead 150 feet stands Henry Van Brunt/William Robert Ware's 1868 *Ether Monument,* which commemorates the 1846 discovery and first use of ether's anaesthetic qualities at Massachusetts General Hospital. Because two doctors claimed to be first, no person's name is given. Oliver Wendell Holmes said it was "a memorial to ether—or either." Near the garden gate halfway to Boylston is Thomas Ball's 1869 equestrian statue of George Washington. Vandals have broken Washington's sword so often that it is now made of easily replaced fiberglass.

As you skirt a small oval garden, a rare Dawn Redwood tree is on your right.

At Newbury across Arlington is the Ritz Carlton Hotel. First opened in 1927, it has housed and fed the well-heeled and famous ever since. From its first floor lounge there is a lovely view onto the garden.

Arlington Street Church (Unitarian) at Arlington and Boylston has a Georgian facade, an interior designed after an Italian church, and 16 Tiffany stained glass windows.

On the path near Boylston's corner is a 1903 statue of Reverend William Ellery Channing, sometimes called the founder of American Unitarianism.

➤Turn left near Arlington and Boylston and follow the path about 0.1 mile to near Boylston and Charles.

Initially on your left is Thomas Ball's 1878 statue of the abolitionist Senator Charles Sumner followed by Theo Alice Ruggles Kitson's 1927 statue of the Polish Revolutionary War General Tadeusz Kosciuszko with the plans for West Point in his hands. An 1899 statue of Union hero Colonel Thomas Cass precedes Daniel Chester French's 1915 statue of the archabolitionist Wendell Phillips.

➤Turn left near Boylston and Charles. Walk about 0.1 mile to and through the garden entrance. Cross Charles at the crosswalk.

➤Re-enter the Common. Turn left and follow the perimeter path about 0.1 mile to near Charles and Beacon.

To your right is Andrzei Pitynski's 1979 cast metal group of five mounted Polish freedom fighters, *The Partisans.*

The 1836 Charles Street Gate near Charles and Beacon is the lone remnant of five such gates connected by a mile-long decorative cast-iron fence—the remaining perimeter section abuts Beacon—that once surrounded the Common. All others were removed during World War

II for use as scrap iron. Found unsuitable for scrap, they were dumped into Boston Harbor.

➤Turn right near Charles and Beacon and continue on the perimeter path about a quarter mile to Beacon and Park.

Across Beacon—called Poor House Lane until 1708— are the early 1820s King's Chapel House bowfronts in the Greek Revival style at Nos. 63–64. The windows in these houses have English glass panes made around 1820; the panes contain manganese oxide which turned violet with exposure to the sun.

The path here is known as Beacon Street Mall. It best reflects the earlier condition of the malls that bordered the Common's other four sides with its original fence and flanking rows of trees. On your left near Charles is the 1930 *Founders Memorial,* which commemorates the 300th anniversary of Boston's founding. John Winthrop's face is said to look suspiciously like that of the then Mayor Curley. On the memorial's right is the 1925 Oneida Football Plaque, marking the site of the very first football game.

As you proceed, you will see, off to your right, the 1877 *Soldiers and Sailors Monument.* A Civil War memorial, it is atop Flagstaff/Powder House Hill—a favorite children's sledding hill and the last remaining of the original four of the Common's hills.

Farther and on your right is the Frog Pond, sole survivor of three Common ponds. A fountain in its center once threw a water jet 90 feet high. A favorite children's supervised wading place on hot summer days, the pond has a wonderful ice skating facility as well as restrooms and food vendors.

William H. Prescott, author of *The Conquest of Mexico* and *The Conquest of Peru,* lived in No. 55 Beacon, Prescott House, open for regular guided tours and now headquarters for the National Society of Colonial Dames in the Commonwealth of Massachusetts.

The finest surviving mansion on Beacon, No. 45 from 1808, is Harrison Gray Otis's last house which—like his earlier two—was designed by famous architect Charles Bulfinch.

The Somerset Club—Boston's oldest, most prestigious private club, founded in 1846 as the Travelers Club—occupies 42–43 Beacon, an 1811 house acquired by the club in 1871.

Henry Wadsworth Longfellow married in No. 39 Beacon, built in 1818. This house and adjoining No. 40, both with violet windows, are now the Woman's City Club.

Bulfinch's 1804 Phillips House in Federalist style at No. 38 was home to Boston's first mayor, John Phillips, and the birthplace of his son, the abolitionist Wendell Phillips.

The double Greek Revival houses at Nos. 33–34 date from 1825. The first is now Boston's official guest house. The other is headquarters for publishers Little, Brown and Company.

At Beacon and Park you will find the *Robert Gould Shaw/54th Massachusetts Regiment Memorial.* The memorial honors and depicts the African-American men of the 54th Massachusetts Regiment and their commander, Colonel Shaw. Originally intended to only depict and honor Colonel Shaw, Shaw's parents insisted the memorial include Shaw's troops. Colonel Shaw and all regimental officers were white, as were those of all black Civil War regiments. The names of slain regimental officers were engraved when it was built; those of the 62 enlisted dead were added only in 1982 on the obverse side.

View the memorial from both sides. It has an Augustus Saint-Gaudens 1897 bronze bas-relief and an architectural

The 54th Massachusetts Regiment

The all-volunteer 54th Massachusetts Regiment was organized in 1863. The 54th was the first black Civil War regiment and the subject of *Glory*—a 1990 film. African-American soldiers were paid less than their white counterparts until late in the war. The men of the 54th refused this lesser pay until Congress relented and retroactively increased it.

The regiment had 900 troops when it marched down Beacon to board transport ships taking it south. The Somerset Club's shades were drawn when it passed—ostensibly to protect carpets from sun damage but believed to reflect members' displeasure with the war and formation of the regiment. Before war's end, 180,000 African-Americans had served the Union.

In July 1865, the regiment—within two months of leaving Boston—advanced bravely, if vainly, against Confederate defenses at Fort Wagner, South Carolina. Outnumbered two-to-one by an enemy defending from prepared fortifications, the result was foreseeable—heavy losses, including the deaths of Colonel Shaw, some regimental officers, and 62 men. Half the men were wounded. One survivor, Sergeant William Carney—the first African-American to receive the Congressional Medal of Honor—grabbed the fallen regimental battle flag and rallied his regiment despite having received three wounds. A photographic reproduction of the flag he saved is in the State House's Hall of Flags.

Those falling at Fort Wagner were buried unceremoniously—officers with men—in a common grave. The Confederates' mass burial of officers with enlisted men was atypical and reflected antipathy toward a black regiment's white officers. When the body of Colonel Shaw—regimental commander, 26-year-old son of a prominent and strongly abolitionist Boston family, and a battle-seasoned veteran slain at Fort Wagner—was identified in the exhumed grave after the war, his family asked that he be returned to the mass grave with his comrades.

setting by architects McKim, Mead and White. Saint-Gaudens took 14 years to complete it. He portrayed each soldier in detail. The memorial is considered Boston's best public art and among the best war memorials anywhere. It was built with funds raised by a citizens' commission. Joshua B. Smith—a former fugitive slave and Shaw household employee as well as a state legislator—played a leading role. The memorial was dedicated in 1897 with Booker T. Washington, heroic Sergeant Carney, and African-American Civil War veterans in attendance.

➤At Park's intersection with Beacon, cross Park and stay right on Beacon for about 0.05 mile to the Athenaeum.

Immediately across Beacon at Park is the State House, Massachusetts's capitol (see Walk 2).

The Boston Athenaeum is located at 10 1/2 Beacon. An 1848 building based on Palladio's Palazzo da Porta Festa in Vicenza, Italy, it was once Ralph Waldo Emerson's home. The Athenaeum is a proprietary library—really an exclusive private club—and art gallery founded in 1807. Here are the personal libraries of George Washington and Henry Knox, America's best collection of detective fiction, and an autobiography, *The Life of a Highwayman,* written by James Allen in 1837 while he waited in prison to be executed (it was bound, at Allen's

Detail, Shaw/54th Massachusetts Regiment Memorial, *Boston Common*

request, in leather made from his own skin). Nonmembers may visit the first two floors. There are guided tours. View the Granary Burying Ground from the fifth-floor terrace. Special events are open to the public.

➤ Retrace your steps to Park and Beacon.

➤ Turn left onto Park and proceed about 0.2 mile to Tremont.

Amory-Ticknor House, No. 9 Park, is an 1803 Bulfinch work. Lafayette stayed here during his 1824 visit. When built, it was Boston's largest house. Thomas Amory went bankrupt just before the housewarming. No one else could afford to maintain it, so it became a boardinghouse for politicians. It now houses Curious Liquids Cafe and No. 9 Park Restaurant.

No. 8 is the Union Club (building circa 1835), the second—in age and prestige—fashionable Boston men's club. Somerset Club members offended by the Southern sympathies of some other members formed the Union Club in 1861.

No. 6 was home to Dr. Jonathan Warren, allegedly the first to use ether during surgery. No. 4 is the 1868 New England Women's Club of Boston, one of the first U.S. women's clubs.

At Park and Tremont stands Park Street Church. Henry James called the 1810 Congregationalist church "the most interesting mass of bricks and mortar in America." Its steeple rises 217 feet. This church had the first Sunday School. In 1819, it sent the first Protestant missionaries to Hawaii, who went from there to proselytize virtually the entire South Pacific. William Lloyd Garrison gave his first speech against slavery here in 1829. The song "America" by Samuel Francis Smith was first publicly sung here in 1831. The American Temperance Society began here in 1826, and the Animal Rescue League, America's first humane society, was organized here in 1889. Gunpowder was stored in its basement during the War of 1812, giving its location the popular name of "Brimstone Corner."

►Turn left onto Tremont and walk half a block to the Granary Burying Ground on your left and enter it. Walk around, then exit as you entered.

Originally part of the Common and adjacent to the site of a granary, Granary Burying Ground, dating from 1660, lies on 2 acres of marshy ground. Cows grazed on the Common, but bulls grazed here at night, providing fertilizer, grass trimming, and security. Among those buried here are Paul Revere, Samuel Adams, John Hancock (maybe, although his hand that signed the Declaration of Independence was taken by graverobbers the night he was buried and some claim that the rest of him was snatched later), Benjamin Franklin's parents, Peter Faneuil, the Boston Massacre martyrs, and the important revolutionaries James Otis and Robert Trent Paine. Few of the 12,000 buried dead are under their own headstones or even ever had one. Some were buried four and more deep because of limited space. The existing stones were rearranged later without regard for the graves' locations. The Egyptian-style gates were designed by Solomon Willard, *Bunker Hill Monument's* architect.

To your left and across Tremont is the Tremont Temple Baptist Church at No. 88—America's first integrated church where Charles Dickens lectured; Abraham Lincoln, Frederick Douglass, Harriet Beecher Stowe, and Daniel Webster spoke; and Will Rogers first said he never met a man he did not like. Farther left on that side, at

School Street, is the Parker House Hotel, America's oldest continuously operating hotel and Boston's first grand hotel. Its combination of comfortable lodging and fine dining was a novelty when it was built in the mid-nineteenth century. Its guests and diners included famous visitors to Boston and virtually every notable Bostonian. The Saturday Club was a monthly gathering here of intellectuals such as Emerson, Holmes, Hawthorne, Dana, Lowell, and Longfellow, as well as special guests such as Dickens and Mark Twain. Willa Cather lived here for a year. Lobby exhibit cases celebrate both famous visitors and the grandest special dinners. The kitchen invented Parker House rolls and Boston cream pie. Ho Chi Minh once worked in the kitchen, and Malcolm X was a waiter.

➤At the Burying Ground gates, turn right, return to Park and Tremont, cross Park, and return to the Park Street T Stop and the start of this walk.

Walk 2

Beacon Hill and Black History Walk

General location: Central Boston.

Special attractions: Historical settings, great architecture, literary and cultural associations, charming antique idiosyncrasies, the State House, and a walk through Boston's black history.

Difficulty rating: Somewhat challenging; cobblestones often provide poor footing over hills and unprotected crossings.

Distance: 2.25 miles.

Estimated time: 70 minutes.

Services: Restrooms and water are available at the Common Visitor Information Center and the African Meeting

Beacon Hill and Black History Walk

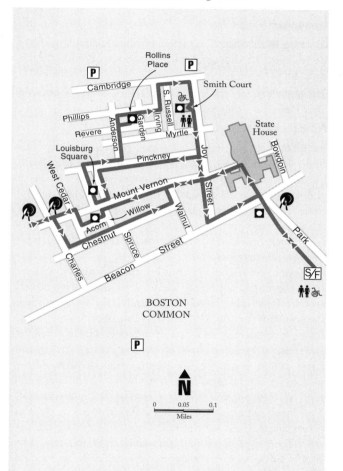

Rollins Place

Cambridge

Smith Court

Phillips

Anderson

Garden

Irving

S. Russel

Myrtle

State House

Revere

Louisburg Square

Pinckney

Joy

Bowdoin

West Cedar

Mount Vernon

Street

Willow

Acorn

Walnut

Chestnut

Charles

Spruce

Beacon

Street

Park

S/F

BOSTON COMMON

N

0   0.05   0.1
Miles

House. Food and drink are available on Park, Bowdoin, Charles, and Cambridge Streets.

Restrictions: None.

For more information: Contact Common Visitor Information Center or Boston African-American National Historic Site.

Getting started: Start at Park Street T Stop on the Common near Park and Tremont Streets. See Walk 1.

Public transportation: See Walk 1.

Overview: Can you visit Boston and *not* see Beacon Hill? Here are interesting old houses—many associated with historical events or literary personages—gas lamps, brick and cobblestone pavements, odd nooks and lanes, and the State House—Massachusetts's old and beautiful capitol. Also here are important historical sites related to Boston's early black community and the national struggle for freedom and civil rights.

Although Beacon Hill has been a fashionable address since the latter eighteenth century, its popularity waned around 1860 when Back Bay was filled. By the 1950s, Beacon Hill was decidedly a neighborhood under stress. Many sections were seedy while others had been razed for government buildings and other new structures. By the latter 1960s, Beacon Hill's prestige—and land values— were again ascendant. There were always "good" and "bad" parts of Beacon Hill. Social climbing was a literal fact! The "best" part has always been that nearest to Beacon Street and highest up the hill. Louisburg Square has always been a place more fashionable than the rest. The North Slope was never quite respectable. It was called "Mount Whoredom" around the Revolution for its unsavory occupants. It was later an area for African-Americans and recent poor immigrants. Residents of the "Flats," at the base of the hill, were generally snubbed by those "above" them. For example, Chestnut Street, when it got to the Flats—where horses were often stabled—was derisively referred to as "Horse Chestnut Street."

The Walk

➤From Park Street T Stop, follow the perimeter path (see Walk 1) 0.15 mile with Park on your right and the Common on your left.

On the Common, Boston's pre–Civil War black community annually celebrated—despite violent opposition by white toughs—the end of the African slave trade. There U.S. slavery's formal abolition was celebrated in a massive public ceremony and Martin Luther King led civil rights rallies.

➤Exit the Common by the stairs next to *Shaw Memorial*—view it from both sides—and cross Beacon Street to the State House grounds.

Two blocks down Beacon, No. 38 at the corner of Walnut Street is the abolitionist Wendell Phillips's birthplace.

Beacon Hill has many houses hidden between houses and tunnel-like passageways to rear gardens. An 1830s building restriction required routes between buildings to be wide enough for a cow and high enough for a boy with a basket on his head. Explore it on your own! Beacon Hill neighborhood extends north to Cambridge, west to the Charles River, south to Beacon, and east to Bowdoin. West of Charles Street, it is aptly known as the "Flats." The neighborhood is in the West End, but brutal "renewal" north of Cambridge made the rest of West End largely uninteresting.

What became Beacon Hill was too hilly to be farmed or lived on. Its three mountains—Pemberton Hill, Mount Vernon, and Beacon Hill, also known by other names—gave Boston an early name, "Tremont" (variously spelled). Atop Beacon Hill, early settlers built a beacon—a raised iron pitch pot to be ignited by watchmen in time of danger. The British razed the original during the Revolution. Its replacement was blown down in 1789. A Charles Bulfinch column commemorating the War for Independence replaced it; a granite and bronze 1898 copy of the column now stands immediately north of the State House, the copy's top level even with Beacon Hill's original peak. In 1811, 60 feet were sliced off Beacon Hill so the property could be developed. This filled 50 acres beyond Causeway Street. Wits say North Station is on Beacon Hill for that reason. Mount Vernon was topped in 1801 and the dirt used to fill Charles Street and the Flats. Pemberton Hill was lowered in 1835.

Freestanding Federal-style mansions were the first buildings. Few survive. A row house style was soon adopted and built on speculation by housewrights, not architects. Even space between freestanding houses was filled with row houses. By the 1830s, Greek Revival—reflected in much of Louisburg Square—was the rage. Victorian facades were sometimes later added to existing structures. True Victorian houses are common on the Flats.

►Walk to the State House.

On the south lawn near the East Wing is Sylvia Shaw Judson's 1959 bronze statue of Mary Dyer. Mary Dyer left Boston with her husband as an adherent of the exiled dissident Anne Hutchinson, converted to Quakerism, came back to Boston in defiance of the 1650s' anti-Quaker laws, and behaved outrageously. She was thrice jailed, was once reprieved from the gallows, but returned yet again to Boston and was hanged in 1660—one of four Quakers executed in Boston around this time. Quakers' executions stopped soon thereafter, but Quakers were publicly whipped until 1665.

Also here are other bronze statues: Daniel Chester French's 1903 Union Civil War General Joseph Hooker, known as "Fighting Joe"—his name was attached to his army's female campfollowers and to their fellow professionals even today; Hiram Powers's 1859 Daniel Webster—New Hampshire–born, a famed orator, U.S. congressman and senator, and U.S. Secretary of State; Emma Stebbins's 1865 Horace Mann—Antioch College's president and best known for his educational theories but also a lawyer and state legislator; Isabel McIlvain's 1988 President John F. Kennedy; Cyrus E. Dallin's 1922 Anne Hutchinson—a Puritan who challenged the early colony's theocratic leadership, she swayed about half the colonists, but when her political protector lost office in 1637 she, her husband, and some of her ardent followers were excommunicated and exiled after which she organized colonies of like-minded people, first in Rhode Island and then on Long Island, where she and her children were killed by natives; and Raymond A. Porter's 1932 Henry Cabot Lodge—a Republican U.S. congressman and senator for 38 years and member of a prominent Brahmin family.

➤Pass through the State House—Massachusetts's capitol—to Mount Vernon Street.

The most prominent and oldest building on Beacon Hill and the finest of Charles Bulfinch's creations is the State House. Bulfinch designed it in 1787. The cornerstone was laid in 1795 by Samuel Adams and Paul Revere. The building was not completed until 1798. Its present marble wings were added in 1914 and 1917. Bulfinch's work is best visible in the first floor Doric Hall and in the second floor Senate Chamber and Reception Room. There were many other additions to and alterations of his original design. It is now ten times the original size. After 1825, the brick was painted—sometimes yellow, sometimes white—until 1928 when the paint was removed to expose the natural brick. Inside are large, ornate rooms filled with artwork depicting Massachusetts's history. The dome—only gilded in 1861 and painted during World War II to prevent its use for orientation by German bombers—is a Boston landmark. Topped by a gilded pine cone to symbolize Massachusetts's wealth derived from its forests—in 1798, Massachusetts administered what is now Maine—the dome was originally of whitewashed wood shingles. The shingles were replaced in 1802 with a gray-painted copper dome made and installed by Paul Revere. The capitol's central front entrance is opened only for a departing governor at the end of his term, a Massachusetts regimental flag returning from a war, or an official visit by a U.S. president.

The flags carried into battle by Massachusetts regiments from the Civil War to Vietnam are in the Hall of Flags. The Sacred Cod, carved from wood and symbolizing the fish's once great importance to Massachusetts, has hung in legislative chambers since 1784. There were at least two earlier models. The legislature will not meet in its absence, which happened for several days in 1933 when the staff of the *Harvard Lampoon* took the Cod and hid it in a closet. Sessions resumed only when the pranksters told where it was hidden.

To your right as you leave the building is the copy of Bulfinch's column/beacon.

►Turn left on Mount Vernon 0.25 mile to and cross Willow Street.

On the stoops of some houses along the way are iron boot scrapers—relics from when the streets were still unpaved. Throughout Beacon Hill are gas street lamps, the occasional hitching post for horses, and brick—and sometimes cobblestone (from the now vanished Charles River shoreline where Charles Street now is)—sidewalks and street pavements. Henry James called Mount Vernon "the only respectable street in America." It is Beacon Hill's widest and greenest street with a setback of 30 feet on parts of the far side of the street.

Julia Ward Howe, writer of "The Battle Hymn of the Republic," lived at No. 32. At No. 55 is Bulfinch's 1804 Nichols House Museum. At No. 57 once resided—at separate times—the politician and orator Daniel Webster and the author Henry Adams. Nos. 50, 56, and 60 are the former stables, designed by Bulfinch, of houses on Chestnut Street. The arched double doors lead to an old wooden cattle ramp and the stable yard, now terraced gardens. The 1837 house at No. 59 is an example of Boston Greek Revival–style architecture. Some houses on its side of the street and elsewhere on Beacon Hill have extensive, well-made iron work brought back as ballast from Seville, Spain, in sailing ships. No. 88 is a former residence of the poet Robert Frost. Harrison Gray Otis's second house—designed by Bulfinch—at No. 85, with cobblestones paving its driveway and courtyard, is the street's grandest freestanding dwelling. No. 87, now headquarters for the Colonial Society of Massachusetts, is an 1806 home (also with cobblestone paving) designed by Bulfinch, but now much altered. Bulfinch intended it for his own residence but sold it due to another of his continual financial difficulties.

Self-taught, Charles Bulfinch was the foremost American architect of post-Revolutionary years. Born in 1763 into a wealthy Boston family, the son of a physician, he graduated from Harvard in 1781, then went to Europe for a two-year grand tour. In Paris he was under Thomas Jefferson's tutelage. He admired what he saw in Europe, particularly the contemporary neoclassic English architecture developed by Robert Adam and Sir William Chambers. Returning to Boston, he pursued no profession but gave "gratuitous advice on architecture" for several years. Far from idle, he designed two state capitols, three churches, two public monuments, a theater, a hotel, and twelve private dwellings. His imprint is on much in and around Beacon Hill. In addition to being a fine, prolific—if impecunious—architect, he was also Boston's chief of police and long the head of its Board of Selectmen. Only 24 years old when he drew the design for Boston's State House (America's finest public building for decades thereafter) he also designed state houses for Connecticut and Maine. He was appointed architect for the federal capitol in 1817, stayed for 12 years, and designed its West Wing. He returned to Boston in 1829, but did no more work here. He died at 81 in 1844. Other Boston examples of his work are the three Otis Gray houses, the Bulfinch Pavilion and Ether Dome, renovated Faneuil Hall, the North End's Saint Stephen's Church, and Harvard's Stoughton and University Halls.

➤Turn left on Willow a half block to Acorn Street.

➤Turn right and walk 0.05 mile down Acorn's middle—staying alert for traffic—to West Cedar Street.

Cobbled, privately owned Acorn is Boston's most photographed street and one of its narrowest. The nine flat-facade brick row houses along this street were built in the

The view up picturesque Acorn Street, Boston's Beacon Hill.

late 1820s by Cornelius Coolidge, perhaps for servants working in nearby houses.

➤ Turn right a half block to and cross Mount Vernon.

The abolitionist Wendell Phillips lived at No. 24 West Cedar. Boston opposed slavery early and strongly. It had a tradition of moral conviction and of religious ministers as community leaders; an honored and self-assured intelligentsia; and a numerous, vocal African-American community. Also important was that it had no economic interest in slavery's perpetuation since plantation agriculture was not profitable here, massive immigration provided cheap labor, and Boston merchants and mariners no longer engaged in the African slave trade. Further, Southerners wanted free trade with Europe while New England favored high tariff protectionism to compel purchases of its manufactured goods, making the two regions natural antagonists. William Lloyd Garrison was among the first to publicly urge slavery's illegalization. He gave Boston's first public abolitionist speech at the Park Street Church on July 4, 1829; formed the New England Anti-Slavery Society at the African Meeting House in 1832; and founded the abolitionist newspaper, *The Liberator,* in 1835. Julia Ward Howe wrote the abolitionist Civil War anthem, "The Battle Hymn of the Republic," here, and her husband, Samuel Gridley Howe, organized a daring abolitionist group—the Committee of Vigilance—made up of prominent Bostonians who prevented the return of fugitive slaves to their masters, assisted fugitive slaves in other ways, and sometimes organized attacks on ships in Boston Harbor to free fugitive slaves. Harriet Beecher Stowe, author of the incendiary *Uncle Tom's Cabin* and "the little lady that started such a big war," as Abraham Lincoln called her, was the daughter of a Boston minister. Boston's black community actively opposed slavery.

➤Turn left on Mount Vernon a short block to and cross Charles Street.

Near the intersection with Charles is the excellent, exotic Lala Rokh Restaurant.

At the corner of Mount Vernon and Charles is the Charles Street Meeting House at 9 Charles. It was built in 1807 by a white Baptist congregation to Boston architect Asher Benjamin's design. When a member in the 1830s invited blacks to attend, he was expelled. He and likeminded people formed the First Baptist Free Church, later the Tremont Temple and America's first integrated church. The Meeting House was purchased in 1876 by Boston's largest black congregation. It met there until relocating to Roxbury in 1939. Famed abolitionists who spoke here included William Lloyd Garrison, Wendell Phillips, Charles Sumner, Harriet Tubman, Frederick Douglass, and Sojourner Truth. Langston Hughes gave his last poetry reading here. An original Palladian classical interior was replaced in the 1850s with a Victorian-style interior. The building was moved 10 feet west in the 1920s when Charles was widened. It was converted to office and retail use in 1982.

➤Recross Charles and turn right a block to Chestnut.

Charles stands on filled land made from 1801 excavations of Mount Vernon. Street widening in 1920 robbed most of the buildings on the farther side of their original facades. The street has many fine antique shops, places to eat and drink, and up-market specialty shops. The three-story Greek Revival brick row houses at 121 and 125–135 Charles—among the few largely unaltered buildings that indicate Charles's earlier character—date from the 1820s.

➤Turn left on Chestnut 0.2 mile to Walnut.

Chestnut is among Boston's handsomest residential streets. The coveted Beacon Hill violet windowpanes are found on No. 70B. At No. 57A, at the corner of West Cedar, is the Harvard Musical Association. The building was erected in 1827 and the association formed in 1837. Note the ornamental iron lyre on the West Cedar exterior wall.

Cornelius Coolidge designed many of this street's houses in the 1830s, including that at No. 50 where American historian Francis Parkman once lived. Richard Henry Dana, author of *Two Years before the Mast,* lived at No. 43.

Bulfinch created 29A—with the prized violet windows—in 1800 in a mid-Georgian design. Its incongruous bowfront was the result of 1818 remodeling. Edwin Booth, actor, assassin John Wilkes's brother, and the theatrical toast of Boston, lived here. He skipped town upon hearing of Lincoln's assassination. Nos. 23 and 25, examples of typical Chestnut residential architecture, were built in 1809 in a mixed Federal–Greek Revival style.

The so-called Swan Houses of about 1804 are Nos. 13, 15, and 17. They were designed by Bulfinch for the heiress Hepzibah Swan and given as gifts to her three daughters upon their marriages.

Julia Ward Howe once lived in No. 13 and held meetings of her Radical Club there.

➤Turn left on Walnut a block to Mount Vernon.

➤Turn right on Mount Vernon a block to Joy Street.

➤Turn left on Joy and stay left a block to Pinckney Street. Joy, laid out in 1661, is among Boston's oldest streets.

➤Turn left on Pinckney 0.2 mile to the entrance to Louisburg Square on your left.

Pinckney traditionally divided black from white Beacon Hill. John Winthrop outlawed slavery in Boston in

1630. Nevertheless, by 1638 African slaves were landed in East Boston and sold at auction. Boston's merchants and ships were important parties in the so-called "triangular trade" in African slaves. By 1705, more than 400 slaves lived in Boston, but there was also a community of free blacks. African-Americans played significant roles in the revolutionary struggle around Boston. Crispus Attucks, the first martyr of the Boston Massacre, was black. African-Americans were Patriot soldiers, sometimes enlisting as free men and other times being freed by their Patriot masters upon their enlistment or following their service. When British officers, officials, and Tory supporters—mostly people of wealth—evacuated Boston, they effectively manumitted their abandoned slaves. In 1783, slavery in Massachusetts was abolished under a case decided by Judge William Cushing. In the first federal census of 1790, Massachusetts was the only state with no slaves. Even with national independence and personal freedom, black Bostonians had limited rights. For example, they were not permitted to freely walk across the Common until July 6, 1836. Boston's black community was initially concentrated in the North End. Many African-American graves are in Copp's Hill Burying Ground. By the early nineteenth century, blacks had largely shifted—encouraged by the African Society—to better quarters on Beacon Hill. At that time Boston's free black community was the United State's largest, as much as 4 percent of Boston's total population. Some were immigrants from the Caribbean and elsewhere. Around World War I, blacks gravitated to the South End and Roxbury, where there is still a large concentration of African-Americans and immigrants of various African heritages.

Henry David Thoreau once lived at 4 Pinckney.

George Middleton, an African-American who served in the Revolutionary War as leader of the all-black Patriot unit known as Bucks of America, lived at 5–7 Pinckney. He built this house in 1797, the oldest Beacon Hill home built by and for the use of an African-American.

Louisa May Alcott lived at No. 20.

No. 24 is the House of Odd Windows, an 1884 carriage house renovation by Ralph Waldo Emerson's nephew, William Emerson. No two of its many windows facing the street are alike.

Nathaniel Hawthorne once roomed in No. 54. The author John P. Marquand lived at No. 57.

The seemingly unremarkworthy house at No. 56 is interesting only were you able to be inside it. It is squeezed between its neighboring houses and follows the contours of their walls. It starts with a typical width facing the street but narrows to a point at its opposite end.

An 1846 brick row house built for George S. Hillard at 62 Pinckney is one of several white-owned Beacon Hill houses with hidden chambers for hiding fugitive slaves. Its chamber was discovered by workmen repairing the house in the 1920s. Possibly Mr. Hillard did not know his home held fugitive slaves since his wife was the avid abolitionist. A black slave escaping his or her master and fleeing to a state outlawing slavery could once generally rely on being protected by the law and popular opinion from a return to servitude. Systematic help given escaped slaves involved assisting them to flee slave states to free states. With 1850's Fugitive Slave Act, a federal law legally compelling any fugitive slave captured anywhere to return to his or her master and slavery, those—both black and white—in free states opposing slavery and assisting escaped slaves had to hide escapees from bounty hunters and law officers until the fugitives could get to freedom in another country. This led to the creation of the so-called "Underground Railroad," a chain of "safe houses" leading north to Canada. Stations were usually in homes that often included secret rooms and hiding places. Because abolitionist sentiment was strong in Boston and the African-American community here was large and naturally sympathetic to fleeing slaves, Boston became a major passage-point. Many, but not all, Boston stations were on Beacon Hill's North Slope, a traditionally black community. Escaped slaves were less noticeable among the residents, and they received strong popular support. The neighborhood's twisted warren of narrow streets also made escape from bounty hunters relatively easy.

At No. 74 1/2—an entrance under No. 74—is the "sally port"/tunnel entrance to a "hidden house" located in the center of the block.

No. 86 Pinckney was the home of John J. Smith, an African-American who left Richmond, Virginia—where he was born free—for Boston in 1848, was in on the California Gold Rush of 1849, and purchased this home in 1878. He was a Civil War recruiting officer, a state legislator, and a member of the Boston Common Council.

➤Enter Louisburg Square, being careful of traffic, and proceed around it clockwise.

The square is thought to be named for the 1745 attack by the British on the town of Louisburg—the "S" is pronounced—in French-held Canada. It was created in 1826. It is the place where other Beacon Hill residents—themselves living at Boston's most prestigious address—aspire to live. The cobbled road and fenced oval park are owned and maintained by abutting property owners—the first homes association in America. The houses were built generally in the period 1835–1847. Only residents and their guests may park on the square's streets. Each parking space is deeded to an individual owner. The statues, from Italy and placed here in 1850, are of *Aristedes the Just* and *Columbus*. Christmas—celebrated with carolers, bell ringers, lighted candles in windows, and other traditions—has long been an acclaimed square feature. The elaborate wrought-iron work on Nos. 1 and 3 is circa 1846. William Dean Howells, editor of *Atlantic Monthly* and author of *The Rise of Silas Lapham,* lived in No. 4. Louisa May Alcott, author of *Little Women* and other famous novels, lived and died at No. 10. Jenny Lind, the "Swedish Nightingale," was married to her accompanist at Nos. 14–20 in 1852 during her American concert tour. Some claim Reverend Blackstone's wilderness home was near the square.

William Blackstone (or Blaxton), an Anglican divine and a Cambridge University graduate, remained behind in what was to become Boston, with his library of 200 books, after the expedition for which he was chaplain failed and returned home. He became benefactor and unwilling victim of the Puritans dying of thirst in Charlestown. He invited them to join him; they did, took almost all his land, and began telling him what to do. He did not like that, sold out, and left. He returned 20 years later at the age of 60, mounted on his trained white bull. He courted and wed a Boston widow, took her to his farm, and fathered two children before dying at the age of 76 in 1675 in Rhode Island.

➤Exit Louisburg Square onto and cross Pinckney, turn right, and stay left a block across Anderson Street.

➤Turn left on Anderson two blocks to and cross Revere Street.

➤Turn right on Revere and stay left to Rollins Place on your left.

Rollins Place is one of four cul-de-sacs off Revere. The 1843 two-story red brick Greek Revival houses lining this short street were built by John Rollins. The two-story white wooden house with an Ionic portico that closes the end of the street seems out of place. It should. It is no house, but an ornamental facade providing a pleasant vista and preventing the unwary from falling off a sheer 20-foot drop behind it.

➤Retrace your route to Anderson.

➤Turn right on Anderson to Phillips Street.

➤Turn right on Phillips two blocks to and cross Irving Street.

Phillips was prominent as a place of refuge for fugitive slaves. Many stayed in lodging houses along this street, with their bills paid by the Committee of Vigilance.

At 66 Phillips is the 1814—occupied by the Haydens after 1849—Lewis and Harriet Hayden House. Lewis Hayden escaped slavery in Kentucky via the Underground Railroad and became a prominent leader in Boston's abolitionist movement. This home was an important Boston Underground Railroad station. Harriet Beecher Stowe visited here in 1853 where—after already writing *Uncle Tom's Cabin*—she saw her first fugitive slaves. Mr. Hayden was a Civil War recruiter, a state legislator, and a Massachusetts Secretary of State staff member.

The 1919 Vilna Synagogue, which housed the oldest (1814) Boston Jewish congregation when this was a Jewish neighborhood, is at No. 14.

At 2 Phillips is the John Coburn Gaming House, an 1844 gambling house catering to an affluent African-American clientele. Coburn commissioned noted Boston architect Asher Benjamin to design it. Coburn was an active abolitionist, the treasurer of the New England Freedom

Association, a petitioner in the Boston desegregation campaign, and a member of the Committee of Vigilance. He was arrested, tried, and acquitted for the 1851 rescue of the fugitive slave Shadrach and was co-founder and captain in the 1850s of the Massasoit Guards, an African-American military company.

➤Turn left on Irving one block to Cambridge Street.

➤Turn right two blocks to Joy.

➤Turn right and stay right a block to Smith Court.

➤Turn right, walk the short distance to the end of Smith Court, return to Joy, and turn right 0.2 mile to Beacon.

At 46 Joy at the corner of Smith Court is the Abiel Smith School. Built in 1834 with an endowment left by an eponymous white businessman, it was a black grammar school serving students from all Boston and replaced the earlier Meeting House School. African-Americans boycotted it soon after its erection in protest against segregated education. It closed in 1855 with the legislated end of segregated education in Boston.

Prince Hall vainly petitioned Massachusetts's legislature in 1787 to educate black children in state public schools. Black parents who fruitlessly filed petitions for separate schools for their children organized a private community school for African-American children in 1798 in Prince Hall's home at West Cedar and Revere Streets. It was moved to the African Meeting House in 1808. Boston did not establish primary schools for black children until the 1820s.

During 1839–1855, Boston was embroiled in controversy over school desegregation. William C. Nell organized the Equal School Association that boycotted the Abiel Smith School and demanded unsegregated education. Benjamin Roberts tried, but failed, to enroll his daughter in each of five public schools between his home and Smith School in 1848. He sued Boston under an 1845 statute permitting recovery of damages from the city for any child unlawfully denied public school instruction. He lost when the court ruled that there was no proof that Smith School's instruction was inferior to that of other Boston public schools. Language from that ruling, "separate but equal," was later used by the U.S. Supreme Court in its *Plessy v. Ferguson* decision of 1896 in support of school segregation's legality, a case only overturned by *Brown v. The Board of Education* in 1956. Segregation—only practiced in Boston—in Massachusetts public schools was legally prohibited in 1855.

Smith Court is a short dead-end street leading off Joy. Nos. 5, 7, 7A, and 10 are typical black-occupied nineteenth-century homes. No. 3 is an exception. It is a clapboard and woodframe double house with a common entryway that was built in 1799 as a farmhouse. Black families rented here from around 1825. An 1851–1865 boarder was William C. Nell, America's first published black historian, a community activist, and leader in the struggle to integrate Boston's pre–Civil War public schools.

The African Meeting House is at No. 8. Dedicated in 1807, the African Meeting House is the oldest African-American U.S. church building still standing. It was built almost entirely with black labor and with funds raised in both the white and black communities. Prior to its construction, black Bostonians could attend white churches, but had to sit in special balconies and could not vote as members. An African-American preacher, Thomas Paul, had led worship meetings for blacks at Faneuil Hall. With 20 followers, he formed the First African Baptist Church in 1805. A school for African-American children was established here in 1808 and functioned until the Abiel Smith School was built. The Meeting House, often referred to as the "Black Faneuil Hall," was both a place for public worship and for community meetings, including celebrations, political rallies, and anti-slavery activities. William Lloyd Garrison founded the New England Anti-Slavery Society here in 1832. Frederick Douglass, Wendell Phillips, Charles Sumner, and Maria Stewart all spoke here on abolition and women's rights. The men of the 54th Massachusetts Regiment enlisted here. The hall was sold to a Jewish congregation at the end of the nineteenth century and served as its synagogue until acquired by the Museum of Afro-American History (now located here) in 1972. Restored, including the interior to its 1854 design, it is open to the public for tours and special exhibits.

Note the 1830s bowfront houses at 1–5 Joy that are set back 15 feet from the street in accordance with a deed restriction intended to permit the seller of the property to continue to see, unobstructed, from his home his cows on the Common below.

➤Turn left on Beacon and retrace your route to the start.

Walk 3
North End

General location: Central Boston.

Special attractions: Faneuil Hall, Quincy Market, Haymarket Square, historic buildings, monuments and statues, dining and drinking spots, Paul Revere's House, Copp's Hill Burial Ground, Old North Church, and Italian ethnicity and charm.

Difficulty rating: Easy; generally on crowded streets and narrow sidewalks.

Distance: 2 miles.

Estimated time: 1 hour.

Services: Restrooms and water are available at the State Street Visitor Center, Faneuil Hall, and Quincy Market. Food and drink are available throughout.

North End

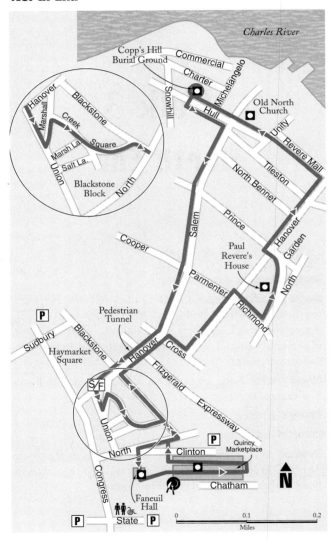

Restrictions: None.

For more information: Contact State Street National Park Service Visitor Center.

Getting started: Start at Union and Hanover Streets. Drivers access this walk from the Central Artery/I-93 exit 24 to North Street, passing under the Central Artery and turning right onto Congress Street. Covered commercial parking (wheelchair accessible, clearance 6 feet) is available at Warren Square on the left on Congress immediately past Sudbury Street. Pedestrian garage access is from Congress. Get to the start by crossing and turning right on Congress a block, crossing Hanover, and turning left to and crossing Union.

Public transportation: Go to Haymarket T Stop, Orange/Green Lines. MBTA bus routes 6/92, 93, 111, 325, 326, 352, 354, 355, 426, 427, 441, 442, 450, and 455 stop at Haymarket Square. Get to the start by walking a few feet to Congress, turning left for half a block, crossing Hanover, and turning left to and crossing Union.

Overview: Most tourists visit the ever-vibrant area around Faneuil Hall/Quincy Marketplace. While there, see quaint, historic North End.

The North End was the place to be in the eighteenth century. The fashionable and important lived here. Here you will find the oldest buildings in Boston and many of Boston's connections with the Revolutionary War, including touchpoints with Paul Revere and his "Midnight Ride." Its old Copp's Hill Burial Ground is fascinating. Much of the North End burned in 1711 and again in 1782. It became unfashionable early in the nineteenth century when the elite abandoned it for Beacon Hill. It then became home for successive waves of newly arrived immigrants—Irish, Jews, and (since the 1890s) Italians—and marginalized groups, including sailors and African-Americans. President Kennedy's forebears were born here, his grandfather, John F. "Honey Fitz" Fitzgerald, on Ferry Street and his mother, Rose, at 4 Garden Street. Rose was baptized in and buried from St. Stephen's. North End was certainly a ghetto and may have fairly been called a slum. It is now identified as "Italian" and plays heavily on that reputation. That is changing. Long a favorite place to come for Italian food, it is now a popular place to live for persons with no Italian ties. A visit on a Friday or Saturday night is magical. Like many beauties, it looks more ordinary on a Sunday morning. Italian parish and social-club patron saint festivals are held virtually every summer weekend. Although everything up to the Old State House is in the North End, the Central Artery/Fitzgerald Expressway separated that section from the North End proper. The isolated part does not partake of the North End's Italian ambiance.

The Walk

➤Start at Union and Hanover. Walk the short distance on Union across Marshall Street, which is on your left.

You will be passing through the Blackstone Block—the inset on the map to this walk and historical markers are guides to this confusing warren—which retains the short, twisting streets, some no more than paths and tunnels, of the seventeenth and eighteenth centuries. It is Boston's oldest commercial block. Benjamin Franklin's father had a chandler shop in the neighborhood.

At 41 Union is Ye Olde Union Oyster House—originally the Capen House circa 1715. An oyster house has operated here since 1826, and the original bar is still in use. This was Daniel Webster's favorite watering hole. The building was earlier used as dry goods and tailor shops with upper floors housing the owner; lodging renters; containing a printing shop for the *Massachusetts Spy,* America's first newspaper; and serving as a classroom for teaching French by the future king of France.

Directly in front of the Oyster House is Stanley Saitowitz's 1993 55-foot *New England Holocaust Memorial* of green glass, granite, stainless steel, and concrete. Each of the six towers represents one of the Nazi death camps. Etched on each tower are a million seven-digit numbers—one for each dead victim of the camps—like those tattooed on concentration camp prisoners for identification. Beneath each tower in a pit 6 feet deep, a gas flame burns—a reminder of the poison gas and incinerators used in the camps and a perpetual memorial to the dead.

➤ Turn left on Marshall to Creek Square.

At 10 Marshall is the circa 1767 Ebenezer Hancock House, probably built by John Hancock's brother. Ebenezer was the Continental Army paymaster. For a time, when France gave money to pay Patriot troops, a critical 2.5 million French silver crowns were stored here.

Across the street and embedded in a wall is the so-called Boston Stone. It was brought from England in 1700 to grind paint pigments and was placed here as a marker in 1737. Despite contrary claims, it was never—like the "London Stone"—the point from which all distances from the city were measured.

➤ Turn right and follow Creek Square's turnings to Blackstone Street.

➤ Turn right on Blackstone to North.

Boston's French

Huguenots—including Paul Revere and Peter Faneuil—were a small but influential part of colonial Boston's population and merchant/artisan class. Huguenots were prosperous, independent-minded French Protestants. They or their forebears were victims of the 1572 St. Bartholomew's Day Massacre when Catholicism's tolerance of Protestantism in France ended with an official blood bath. Many survivors fled. Some—or their descendants—came to Boston.

In 1778, French officers delivered a large sum of French money to finance America's Revolution and pay revolutionary soldiers. Feted often, at one state dinner the cook—aware of peculiar French tastes—served them soup with a boiled frog in each bowl!

Boston knew and was known by the Marquis de Lafayette. In Boston during the Revolution, he made a return visit in 1824. Boston went mad! Streets and other places were named for him and even for "La Grange," his French summer residence. He lies in a Parisian grave under soil from Bunker Hill battlefield.

Liberty Square was named in 1793, not for American liberty, but in honor of the French Revolution. Enthusiasm cooled, but the name stayed.

Residing in Union Oyster House and teaching French to Boston society in the early nineteenth century was the exiled Louis-Philippe under the name M. d'Orleans. He became France's king, briefly, after Napoleon's fall.

Frenchmen in Boston in the late eighteenth/early nineteenth centuries were of contrasting personalities. The wily opportunist Prince Charles Maurice de Talleyrand was a noble and a radical revolutionary; an excommunicated, licentious Catholic bishop; Napoleon's friend, adviser, and betrayer; and orchestrator of the Bourbon monarchy's and fellow Boston-resident Louis-Philippe's restoration. He said he never betrayed a government that had not first betrayed itself. Good John Cheverus from France was a Roman Catholic priest and Boston's first bishop. He was beloved by Catholic and Protestant alike.

➤Turn right on North to and over the crossing to Faneuil Hall.

At the corner of Congress and North nearby are Lloyd Lillie's 1989 bronze double (one standing, one seated) life-size portrait statues of Mayor James Michael Curley. In 1914, Curley became mayor. He ruled Boston for 30 years. He was Irish and proud of it. He came from poverty with little formal education, but was widely read. His admirers regard him as a Robin Hood, but he was divisive, confrontational, and the author of disastrous economic and political policies. His politics were all power for Curley, jobs for the boys, remember your friends, stick your thumb in the Brahmin Yankees' eyes, and squeeze the money-makers. He was four times—never consecutively—mayor of Boston as well as a U.S. congressman, governor, state legislator, and city alderman and councillor. He held his first office in 1904 while in jail. He was elected from jail for his last term as mayor and had to be pardoned by President Truman in 1946 so he could serve.

➤Cross the plaza to and enter Faneuil Hall.

In front of Faneuil Hall is Anne Whitney's 1873 bronze, heroic-sized statue of Samuel Adams, a copy of that in Statuary Hall in the federal capitol. Samuel Adams deserves more credit than anyone else for the Revolution.

He was for independence when few that would later lead the Revolution were. He was an effective orator and demagogue, a chief promoter of the Boston Tea Party, and the organizer of groups of rough agitators that did much to precipitate events that led to hostilities between Britain and the colonies. He was a second cousin of President John Adams and later Massachusetts's governor. He often spoke in Faneuil Hall and from there organized Committees of Correspondence through which Patriots in the colonies shared their thoughts and coordinated their plans. On the base of his statue—Bostonians are frugal!—is the 1976 bronze *Walter Muir Whitehill*—a noted Boston scholar—*Medallion*.

Faneuil Hall was a 1742 gift to the people of Boston by Peter Faneuil. Faneuil was the bachelor heir of a wealthy but difficult uncle. A condition of his inheritance was that he never marry. His brother was disinherited because he married before first gaining his uncle's approval. Peter was seemingly willing to accept that condition. He named one of his ships *The Jolly Bachelor* and was jolly himself. He is said to have died of "too much good living." The hall was to be used as a public market. Bostonians accepted his gift by the close margin of seven popular votes. To appease opponents, Faneuil added a second-floor meeting hall with the market on the ground floor. The building burned in 1761 but reopened in 1763. It was in the meeting hall that the hall earned its title, "Cradle of Liberty"—a tarnished reference since Faneuil's money came partly from the African slave trade. At the hall, Boston colonials protested many British acts and perceived outrages. After the Boston Tea Party, the British banned further meetings in the hall, quartered troops there, and used the hall as a theater for staging amateur entertainments.

After the Revolution, the hall continued as the site for public debate. Abolitionists Wendell Phillips, William Lloyd Garrison, and Frederick Douglass spoke—as did Jefferson Davis in a defense of slavery. Other topics included women's suffrage and anti-alcohol temperance. The hall is twice as large now as in Revolutionary days—the result of an 1806 enlargement by Bulfinch. Most of the interior is his as well. A balcony and third floor were added but three original outer walls were kept. The hall was entirely rebuilt in 1898 using noncombustible materials.

The grasshopper weathervane atop Faneuil Hall has been there since 1742—barring being knocked off by an earthquake in 1755, falling off during the 1761 fire, and being insect-napped in 1974. Always it has been put back, good as new. Shem Drowne, creator of other windvanes still seen around Boston, made it.

On the meeting room wall hangs a life-size portrait of Daniel Webster. Commissioned by King Louis-Philippe of France in 1842—he and Webster were fellow habitues of Union Oyster House—it hangs here because the king was deposed before he could take delivery.

Since 1746 in Faneuil Hall and since 1806 in the meeting room on the third floor has been the Armory Museum of the Ancient and Honorable Artillery Company, called "the Ancients." The Ancients were formed in 1637, the oldest American militia organization. The Ancients' only services as a unit were in a skirmish with the natives under Myles Standish and in suppressing Shay's Rebellion in 1787. Today they are a ceremonial and honorary organization.

➤Leave Faneuil Hall. Cross the plaza to and enter the Quincy Marketplace buildings.

Nearby is Lloyd Lillie's 1985 bronze, life-size seated statue of Red Auerbach, longtime coach and manager of the Boston Celtics.

Quincy Marketplace, named after Mayor Josiah Quincy, dates from 1825. It was designed by Alexander Parris in the Greek Revival style using Quincy granite. It was completely renovated for a different purpose in 1977 and consists of three buildings, a central Quincy Market Building and flanking North and South Market Buildings. There are street performers in adjacent plazas, a voluminous food court in the Quincy Market Building, and shops selling many things in the adjacent buildings. There is always a large crowd. The market is a mecca for tourists and a place where something is always happening. Upstairs in the Quincy Market Building is, since 1827, a unique Boston institution—Durgin-Park Restaurant.

➤Come out of North Market Building, cross Clinton Street to North Street, stay right, return to Blackstone, and turn left onto Blackstone to Hanover.

You will pass the Haymarket, an open-air market since Boston's early years—no longer selling hay—and a lively place on Fridays and Saturdays for pushcart vendors and shopkeepers in adjacent buildings. Check it out!

On the pavement at Hanover near Haymarket Square are Mags Harries's 1976 bronze inserts of assorted sizes in an area 55 by 10 feet. Called *Asaroton (Unswept Floor)*, the name refers to a second century B.C. Greco-Roman floor mosaic technique. The castings are of garbage and other items found on the street.

➤Turn right on Hanover and follow the pedestrian tunnel under Fitzgerald Expressway to and cross Cross Street (press the button for protected crossings). This is the "real" North End and prime "Big Dig" territory (see page 16), so stay flexible.

➤ Turn right on Cross a block to Hanover Street.

➤ Turn left on Hanover 0.1 mile to and cross Richmond Street.

Hanover was the main street joining the North End with the rest of Boston peninsula and is still North End's main commercial street. Many Italian shops and restaurants are located along it.

Langone's Funeral Home at No. 383 was where Nicola Sacco and Bartolomeo Vanzetti, two Italian-born anarchists convicted—perhaps falsely, which was why they became a *cause celebre*—of murdering two men and stealing a payroll in 1920, were laid out with a huge funeral cortege extending the length of Hanover following their executions in 1927.

➤ Turn right on Richmond a block to North.

➤ Turn left on North and stay left 0.1 mile as North turns to North Square and then to Garden Street until you come to Prince Street.

On North Square are the Paul Revere House (No. 19), the Pierce-Hichborn House (No. 29, 1710), and the Mariners' House (No. 11, 1838).

The Paul Revere House was built around 1677; it is Boston's oldest surviving frame house, but has been repeatedly remodeled and modified since that time. Revere bought it in 1770 when it was almost a century old and stayed there until 1800. Restored to its appearance at approximately the time Revere lived there, it contains some of his furnishings. Of French Huguenot extraction, a talented artisan, and an ardent worker for independence, Paul Revere (1735–1818) is best known today because of Longfellow's poem, "Paul Revere's Ride." He was an early, active, and brave Patriot. His widely distributed, dramatic engraving of the Boston Massacre did much to transform

The Paul Revere House, Boston's North End.

a relatively minor incident, for which both sides were blameworthy, into incendiary popular resentment against the British. He repeatedly rode long distances carrying messages of great importance among Patriot leaders. Revere is praiseworthy for his silver and gold work, and his entrepreneurialism—he made copper ship hull sheathing, put a copper dome on the State House, made false teeth, and owned a brass foundry that cast the bells found in many old New England churches. In 1795, he organized America's first multi-trades "labor union," and his qualities as a husband (twice), father (16 times), and citizen are also noteworthy. Revere should be famous for many things, and what he did—or attempted to do—on his midnight ride was important, but popular opinion has confused the facts. On the night of April 18, 1775, when he made that ride after seeing the two lights from the Old North Church steeple, he was not the sole rider sent to alert the Patriot militia in the countryside and Patriot leaders in Concord. John Dawes also rode that night. Robert Newman gave the signal from the steeple tower. Revere was caught by a British patrol before he reached Concord. A companion, Dr. Samuel Prescott, who Revere fortuitously encountered on the road in Lexington, knew the shortcuts and made it there. Neither Dawes nor Prescott, let alone Newman, is recognized by Americans. Each took risks and accomplished deeds that night equal to Revere's.

➤Turn left on Prince a short distance to and cross Hanover.

➤Turn right on Hanover three blocks to and enter Paul Revere Mall—known locally as the "Prado"—on your left.

Across Hanover from the mall is Charles Bulfinch's 1804 St. Stephen's Church. It is Bulfinch's only surviving

Boston church. Revere made its bell and dome. Originally called New North Church and Congregational, then Unitarian, since 1862 it has been Roman Catholic because the influx of immigrants and the departure of earlier congregants made this transfer sensible. The church was moved back 16 feet and raised 5 feet in 1870 with the widening of Hanover. It was restored in 1964 to its earlier style and dropped to its earlier elevation.

►Follow the mall two blocks across Unity Street and right along Hull Street to Salem Street and Old North Church.

Bronze plaques along the mall's walls tell of North End people and places. In the mall is Cyrus Dallin's 1885—but only cast in 1940—equestrian statue of Paul Revere. Pleasant gardens are in back of Old North Church.

Christ Church, Episcopal, better known as Old North Church, is still a functioning church. Maybe it is not "the Old"—some say the title goes to Second Church, called "Old North," on North Square, which dates from 1667 and was destroyed by the British for firewood in 1776. Old North Church is famous as the place from whose steeple Revere received his signal of "one if by land, two if by sea" and whose news he carried with him on his Midnight Ride. But maybe it was not. Some historians claim the signal was sent from Second Church. Old North Church was designed in 1723 by William Price. It is Boston's oldest church building and second oldest Anglican parish. Built of red brick, it is modeled on London's St. Andrew's-by-the-Wardrobe in Blackfriar. Its peal of eight bells—America's oldest set—was cast in England in 1744 and rung by Paul Revere and six friends who organized a group of bellringers. It is still rung. The church's 175-foot steeple has been knocked down several times by hurricanes. Each time it has been rebuilt. The weathervane on top, made by deacon Shem Drowne who also made that atop Faneuil Hall, is the original. So are the salvaged and reinstalled steeple glass panes through which Newman's lanterns shone. This steeple may also be the site of the first American manned flight. In 1757, John Childs leapt—repeatedly by some accounts—from it wearing something like a parachute and landed, alive and well, several hundred yards away.

Each April 18 evening, lanterns are hung in Old North Church's belfry by descendants of Paul Revere and Robert Newman. Inside, note Christian Gullager's 1815 marble bust of George Washington made from an oil portrait by the same artist for which Washington sat. The high box pews were owned by individual parishioners and designed to retain heat from hot bricks or coals placed on the floor on winter days. The brass chandeliers were first lit on Christmas Day 1724. The four cherubim on the organ are the 1746 gift of a sea captain and privateer who captured them from a ship bound for Quebec. The clock at the back, made by two parishioners in 1726, is still running.

➤Exit the church, cross Salem, and follow Hull a block and a half to Copp's Hill Burial Ground on the right.

In the late eighteenth century, the northeastern base of Copp's Hill was called "New Guinea" and was home to most of Boston's African-Americans.

➤Enter, view Copp's Hill Burial Ground, depart, and cross over and turn left on Hull a block to Salem.

The oldest North End cemetery, Copp's Hill Burial Ground's first burial is dated 1660. More than 10,000 people are buried here, about 1,000 of them African-Americans in a reserved western portion. There is a monument to the blacks buried here. A broken column marks the grave of Prince Hall, an African-born Revolutionary soldier, an early Boston African-American leader, and founder of the black Masonic order.

Increase, Cotton, and Samuel Mather are buried here. The Mathers were a dynasty of religious leaders—most notably Richard the father, who came to Boston in 1635 and was pastor of the Dorchester Church; his son Increase; his grandson Cotton; and his great-grandson Samuel—whose power in Boston lasted four generations and a century and a half. They intermarried with Cotton daughters and widows to cement their primacy among Boston clerics. Eleven of Richard's sons were religious ministers. Among them they published more than 500 works. Increase was a cleric, scholar, Harvard University president, and political spokesman who was sent to England in 1692 by Massachusetts Bay's colonists to negotiate the return of their rescinded royal charter which was their assurance of independence. He returned without the charter but with a far better deal than could have been hoped. Cotton was a precocious—entering Harvard at 12—but immodest child. His scholarly discoveries were sometimes extraordinary, like his report to London's Royal Society that he had determined that Satan understood English, Latin, Greek, and Hebrew, but not the Indian language. He was capable both of great piety and of persecuting a woman for being a witch and assuring that she was hanged for it. Cotton's son, Samuel, was a great scholar but an indifferent preacher. The Mather dynasty ended with Samuel's death in 1785.

Excellent views of Boston Harbor, Charlestown, Bunker Hill, the Charlestown Navy Yard, and *Old Ironsides* may be had from the hill. Copp's Hill Terrace, a granite promontory off Charter Street at the edge of the burial ground, leads down to Commercial Street and the waterfront. On January 15, 1919, a North End storage tank holding 2.5 million gallons of liquid molasses burst. The 15 foot-high flood of thick goo had such force it destroyed buildings and the elevated railroad in its path, still traceable along Commercial from Copp's Hill, and moved so quickly—in January, so so much for the old adage—that 21 persons and many horses were killed and over 50 persons were injured. Revere had a foundry for church bells at the corner of Commercial and Foster Streets and the USS *Constitution* was built at Constitution Wharf at 409 Commercial.

Boston's narrowest house is No. 44 Hull at 9.5 feet. The owner built it for spite to spoil the view of a neighbor who lived in the lot behind it.

➤Turn right 0.3 mile on Salem to and through the tunnel under Fitzgerald Expressway continuing as Hanover to Union.

Salem after 1850 was largely Jewish. The early twentieth-century entertainer, Sophie Tucker, lived as a child at No. 22.

➤You are across the street from the start and near your transportation.

Walk 4

Back Bay

General location: Near central Boston.

Special attractions: Great architecture, statuary, shopping, and people watching, and wide, tree-shaded Commonwealth Avenue Mall.

Difficulty rating: Easy; flat, well-paved sidewalks and protected crossings.

Distance: 2.25 miles.

Estimated time: 70 minutes.

Services: Restrooms and water are available at the Boston Public Library. Food and drink are available throughout, particularly on Boylston and Newbury Streets.

Restrictions: None.

For more information: Contact the Greater Boston Convention and Visitors Bureau Center.

Back Bay

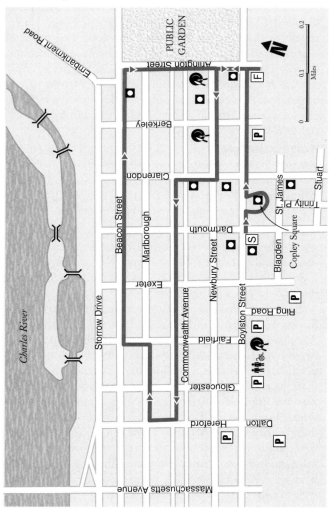

Getting started: Start at Boston Public Library, Boylston and Dartmouth Streets. Drivers access this walk from the I-90 exit 22 onto Huntington Avenue and left onto Dartmouth to Boylston. Covered commercial parking (wheelchair accessible, clearance 6 feet) is available at Prudential Center (right side of Boylston at Fairfield Street) by continuing on Dartmouth, turning left onto Newbury, left onto Gloucester Street, and left onto Boylston. Pedestrian garage access is from Boylston. Get to the start by turning right on Boylston for two blocks to Dartmouth.

Public transportation: Arrive at Copley Square T Stop, where you will literally emerge out of the side of Boston Public Library, and return via Arlington T Stop, Green Line, at Arlington and Boylston. MBTA bus routes 9, 10, 55, and 202 stop at Copley Square, half a block from the start.

Overview: This is an easy, enjoyable, and interesting urban walk. The neighborhood is beautiful, the architectural styles grand and varied, the ambiance pleasant, the historical and literary connections interesting, and the shopping marvelous. What is not to like?

Back Bay runs east to Boylston, north to Arlington Street, west to Storrow Drive, and south to Massachusetts Avenue. East-west streets, named for English dukedoms, begin with alphabetically sequential letters from north to south. Back Bay was a shallow bay. A stench of sewage arose after a dike extended Beacon Street across it and Boston's dumped wastes were no longer removed by the tides. Needham's sand dunes were hauled to Back Bay and dumped from 1857. About 450 new acres emerged over 30 years, starting at the Public Garden and moving south to solid ground near Kenmore Square. Building occurred as land was created. There is a progression of architectural styles from north to south—starting with French forms, moving to English patterns, and on to highly eclectic styles. Only residential buildings and churches were authorized, but Boylston and Newbury soon became commercial centers. Due to soggy, unstable soil, many buildings are built on multiple wooden pilings driven through the fill and into firm ground. Although many homes are grand and were specially built, most were speculative construction by developers. With buildings too large for a modern family, people later abandoned the neighborhood. Houses were divided into rental apartments or were sold to local colleges. Renewed prosperity and renovating buildings for condominiums has again made Back Bay Boston's place to be.

The Walk

➤Start at Boston Public Library, Boylston and Dartmouth. You are two blocks from Prudential Center—known locally as "the Pru," a center for shopping and dining. A block farther is the John J. Hynes Civic Auditorium.

On the library, note first the T stop entrance's 1914 wrought-iron design. "New" Old South Church (United Church of Christ) is across Boylston. Built in 1874 in Italian Gothic style, its puddingstone exterior is highly ornamented and detailed. It is noted for its readily visible, tall campanile and Venetian lantern—the central red tower with oxidized copper roof. The tower was originally 246 feet tall, but began to lean soon after construction. By 1931, it was a yard out of plumb and a public danger; in 1940, it was taken down and replaced with the present tower.

Boston Public Library is a great American architectural work. Examine it inside and out. It was founded in 1848 and opened in 1854. It was the first large U.S. city library freely available to the general public. Starting in 1887, Charles McKim was in charge of designing and building the library. He recruited famed artists and artisans, such as Augustus and Louis Saint-Gaudens, Daniel Chester French, Pierre Puvis de Chavannes, the pre-Raphaelite Edwin Austin Abbey, and the painter John Singer Sargent. McKim's Renaissance Revival design was patterned on Italian Renaissance palazzi, particularly on Alberti's San Francesco in Rimini, Italy, and Labrouste's Bibliotheque Sainte Genevieve in Paris, France. A budget of $450,000 grew to $2.5 million. Completed in 1895, an addition by the architect Philip Johnson was added in 1971. The bronze doors representing *Music and Poetry, Knowledge and Wisdom,* and *Truth and Romance* are by French. Above them is carved, "Free for All." The entrance is flanked by Bela Pratt's statues representing *Science* and *Art.* The marble interior stairway is guarded by Augustus Saint-Gaudens's stone lions and its walls are covered by de Chavannes's murals of *Good and Bad Tidings.* Abbey's *Quest of the Holy Grail* murals are on the book request room's walls. Sargent's *Triumph of Religion* with murals representing *Judaism* and *Christianity* cover a third-floor gallery. There is a lovely Italianate central courtyard. On the facade are carved the names of famous men of learning—allegedly originally arranged so the first letters of each spelled the architectural firm's name but reordered when this was discovered. Fliers are available by de Chavannes, Sargent, and Abbey—assisted by Henry James—describing their works. The library houses excellent collections of rare and old books.

McKim, Mead and White (MMW) was an architectural firm in New York City, but it had good Boston connections and designed a number of important Boston buildings. Charles Follen McKim, the lead MMW partner, was a draftsman in H. H. Richardson's office, worked on the First Baptist Church and Trinity Church under Richardson, and was the principal architect on the Boston Public Library—his best creation in Boston and perhaps of his career. Although the library's cost rose to $2.5 million, for its eight years' work MMW received a fee of merely $22,000. Stanford White—the "White" in MMW's name—had apprenticed for several years with Richardson and worked on the Trinity Church tower. He is best known today—and became notorious in his time—for being murdered at a theater by the demented husband of his former mistress.

➤Cross Dartmouth and go half a block on Boylston to and enter Copley Square to your right.

Copley Plaza Hotel is across the square. The Hare and Tortoise statues and the Boston Marathon markers (see Walk 14B) are near your path.

John Hancock Tower by I. M. Pei and Partners, to your left across the square, beautifully reflects clouds and Trinity Church from certain angles. At 62 stories and 740 feet, it is New England's tallest building. Covered with reflective glass—13 acres of it—when it was built in 1964, 65 of its 500-pound panes burst and tumbled onto the pavement (and pedestrians) below, creating both consternation and danger. Correction has been difficult and costly.

Beyond John Hancock Tower is the "old" John Hancock Tower—now the John Hancock Building, locally famed for the weather beacon at its tip. The beacon is lit at night and changes color in keeping with this doggerel, "Steady blue, clear view; Flashing blue, clouds are due; Steady red, rain ahead; Flashing red, snow ahead—except in summer when it means the Red Sox are rained out."

Trinity Church is in the square's center. Trinity Church (Episcopal) parish was founded in 1733. The church is from 1875. Its portico and front tower peaks were revised in the 1890s based on the Church of Saint Trophime in Arles, France. The architect was the later famous H. H. Richardson. The site presented challenging problems. Small, triangular, sodden, unstable, and abutted on every side by streets, it would be the focus of every passerby because of its location. The design is basically Romanesque—in the style of the Auvergne region of central France—using a compact Greek cross footprint with a large central tower inspired by Spain's Cathedral of Salamanca. The church rests on 4,500 wooden pilings—covered by huge granite pyramids—driven through fill into solid land. The auditorium ground plan is three squares—one the apse, the second the crossing, and the third the nave. From apse to facade it is 160 feet in length. The transepts' width is 120 feet. At their highest point, the ceilings are 63 feet—103 feet for the tower, which rises to an outer height of 211 feet from ground to finial top. The major building material was very red granite; red sandstone was used for the trim; and semiglazed red tiles were incorporated into the design—all of which provide a very colorful appearance. The interior is equally dramatic. John La Farge executed Richardson's Trinity Church interior design, assisted by young assistants Augustus Saint-Gaudens and Louis Comfort Tiffany—both later famous. Some claim Tiffany copied his stained glass techniques from La Farge. Noteworthy is the painted—dull terra cotta, gold, and blue-green—plaster applied using newly developed techniques that cover the church's interior granite surface. The Baptistery and North Transept north wall—over the gallery—stained glass windows were made

Copley Square with Trinity Church, Boston's Back Bay.

by the acclaimed Sir Edward Burne-Jones and William Morris. Trinity Church was built to serve Phillips Brooks, its first rector and later a bishop. He wrote the Christmas carol, "O, Little Town of Bethlehem." The church's many uses of his name and image were added after his death. Tours are given after the end of Sunday services. Pamphlets describing the church are available.

Henry Hobson Richardson is considered by many to be the most influential nineteenth-century American architect. He was architect of Trinity Church and of many other buildings and structures in Boston and elsewhere. Although Trinity Church brought him fame and influence and is rated among the ten best American buildings by almost every critic, Richardson thought at least two of his other works were better. Richardson was from Louisiana, abandoned pursuit of a military career because of a stutter, graduated from Harvard, and was 34 and living in New York City when invited to bid on the Trinity Church commission. The building of the church took five years and cost $750,000—almost three times budget, but Richardson received only $7,218.90 for his work.

➤Exit Copley Square as you entered, turn right on Boylston, and walk 2.5 blocks to Arlington.

On your right at 500 Boylston is Philip Johnson's 1988 "new" New England Life Building. Next to it is Robert A. M. Stern's 1991 222 Berkeley Street. They were to have been twin towers, both like the former, but community opposition compelled award to Stern of the design for the latter. The result is an unhappy pairing of buildings, each interesting in its way.

Across Boylston is the 1940 "old" New England Life Building at 501. In its lobby is a diorama of an early native fish weir found when the building's site was excavated.

The teddy bear statue in front of F.A.O. Schwartz's is no ordinary teddy bear, not even an ordinary F.A.O. Schwartz one. It is 12 feet high and made of *solid* bronze.

On your right is the Beaux Arts–influenced 1905 Berkeley Building at 420 Boylston, a building often condemned by experts but a popular favorite. Designed by Desire Despredelle, a French architect on MIT's School of Architecture faculty, its lacy facade is enameled terra cotta and glass applied to a lightweight steel frame.

Women's Educational and Industrial Union (WEIU), established "to teach immigrant women millinery and culinary skills," is at 356. The golden swan in front reflects that the 1877 date of WEIU's founding was the same year the first Public Garden Swan Boats appeared. WEIU is a delightful place to shop for fine handmade items while supporting its program.

➤Turn left on Arlington and walk a block to Newbury. The Public Garden is on your right. Immediately on your left is Arlington Street Church, Back Bay's first public building and the "mother church" of American Unitarianism (note King's Chapel's competing claim).

As the Federal Street Church congregation—founded in 1729—it was once led by the abolitionist preacher William Ellery Channing. One of his pulpits is here. The church was designed by Arthur Gilman, designer of Back Bay's overall plan and Old City Hall's primary architect. It is made of brownstone, has a Georgian facade inspired by the works of Christopher Wren, and rests on almost 1,000 wooden pilings. It has an airy, white, Italianate interior modeled on Genoa's Church of the Annunziata and many Tiffany stained glass windows.

➤Turn left on Newbury two blocks to and cross Clarendon Street.

Newbury is Boston's premier shopping street. Across Newbury is the Ritz Carlton Hotel, long a prestigious place to stay, drink, and dine.

On your right at 15 is Emmanuel Church (Episcopal), built in 1862 and enlarged in 1899. It was the first Back Bay Gothic Revival church and the first to use puddingstone. A Bach cantata is part of each 10 A.M. Sunday service. The Leslie Lindsey Memorial Chapel—she married in the church and died on her honeymoon when the ship *Lusitania* was torpedoed and sunk by a German U-boat—was added in 1920–1924. The ornamental ironwork, the high altar, and the stained glass of the chapel are of special interest.

At 234 Berkeley Street is Louis, now a fashionable clothing store with a wonderful restaurant, Cafe Louis; it was the Museum of Natural History when built in French Academic style in 1862.

At 67 Newbury is the Gothic Revival, puddingstone, 1866 Church of the Covenant (Presbyterian), with 40 Tiffany stained glass windows, a Favrile glass lantern inside from the Tiffany Chapel at the 1893 Chicago World's Fair, and a 236-foot ornate spire.

On your right at the corner of Clarendon is Richardson's 1879 Trinity Church Rectory. Look a block farther down Newbury to the corner of Dartmouth for a glimpse of Joshua Winter's 1991 Newbury Street Mural. A key to the 50 famous Bostonians depicted is available from the Du Berry Restaurant on whose wall it is painted.

➤Turn right on Clarendon a block to Commonwealth Avenue.

Clarendon is a good street for noting architectural embellishments such as panel brickwork, incised line decoration, and glazed tiles.

On your left at Commonwealth is Richardson's 1871 First Baptist Church. Richardson first used the Romanesque form here in preparation for Trinity Church. Galleries were added in 1884 to reduce echoes in the sanctuary. The church is made of randomly laid Roxbury puddingstone—a favorite material for public buildings in the Back Bay because of its warm, rich hues. Look at the walls to see why it is called puddingstone. Small, embedded pebbles in the stone are like raisins in a boiled pudding. The virtually freestanding monumental bell tower is distinctive. The decorative frieze at the top is the work of Frenchman Frederic-Auguste Bartholdi, who sculpted the Statute of Liberty. Trumpeting angels at each corner of the tower gave rise to the church's nickname, "Church of the Holy Beanblowers." The characters in the frieze are modeled on famous Boston personages of the time, including Longfellow, Emerson, Hawthorne, and Sumner. The congregation that built the church spared no expense. It went bankrupt in the process and sold the completed structure to a Baptist congregation that still has it.

➤Cross to Commonwealth's center mall and turn left five blocks to Hereford Street.

The mall, 100 feet wide and almost a mile long with buildings set back 20 feet from the road, was the 1858 design of Arthur Gilman. It was incorporated into Olmsted's Emerald Necklace (see Walk 9). It is bordered by some of Back Bay's grandest buildings. Numerous sculptures are along it, including those depicting Alexander Hamilton, William Lloyd Garrison, and Samuel Eliot Morison.

At 152 Commonweatlth is the Chilton Club, a very prestigious women's club founded in 1910 and named for Mary Chilton—the only *Mayflower* passenger to live in Boston and the first passenger to alight. At the corner, 306 Dartmouth is the 1872 Ames-Webster Mansion. Once a grand mansion but now offices, it retains some elaborately ornamented interiors. Across Commonwealth at 160 is the 1871 Hotel Vendome in the French Second Empire style. It was part of a short-lived nineteenth-century Back Bay enthusiasm for the equivalent of condo living, was Boston's premier luxury hotel but is now offices, and suffered a huge 1972 fire that resulted in the death of several firemen commemorated by a memorial in the mall nearby.

J. H. Besarick created 172 Commonwealth with his characteristic foliate carvings. Look for other examples. Another "French flat" multiple residence is 191, the 1872 Hotel Agassiz, at Exeter. Note the extensive use of custom-made terra cotta at 195. The Saint Botolph Club, established in 1881 for artists, writers, and professional men, is at 199, an MMW 1890 Federal Revival building. The Mason House at 211, only moderately interesting outside, has elaborate Queen Anne interiors and was the scene of piano performances by many greats, including Paderewski and Rubenstein. MMW is also responsible for the Algonquin Club of 1887 at 217, a palatial businessmen's club and one of the few Back Bay buildings with its original owner and serving its original purpose. At 287 is the International Institute—"supporting and assisting foreign residents"—in what was an 1892 private mansion with classic Greek touches. It retains Codman's 1904 interiors.

Nearing Hereford, to your left and across Commonwealth at 314, is the 1889 Burrage Mansion. Inspired by

Of Interest

Boston's Interior Designers and Decorators

Much is made of Boston buildings' outside designers. Less is said of their interior designers and artisans. Many Boston places were more beautiful within than without. Some interiors remain largely or entirely intact. A few, such as Fisher College at 118 Beacon or Emerson College's Abbott Library at 150 Beacon, may be viewed generally or by special arrangement.

While some interior designers were specialized artisans and took no responsibility for overall interior design, one name stands out—Ogden Codman, Jr. A Boston Brahmin and architect, he designed and decorated mansions around the country and around the world. Many know his creative interiors in the magnificent summer homes in Newport, Rhode Island. He was responsible for the interiors of some of Boston's grandest homes and other buildings of the 1880s. He co-authored with Edith Wharton a classic book on interior decoration called *The Decoration of Houses*.

the French chateau Chenonceaux, it is heavily ornamented in and out, is atypically—for Boston—ostentatious, and is now a retirement home.

➤Turn right on Hereford a block to Marlborough Street.

On the corner to your right at 32 Hereford is the 1886 MMW John F. Andrew Mansion in the Italian Renaissance Revival style. Many original interiors are maintained by the MIT fraternity occupying it. Across the street at 40 is the site of a former home of Fanny Farmer's School of Cookery.

➤Turn right on Marlborough two blocks to Fairfield.

Perle Mesta, the fabled Washington "hostess with the

mostest," lived at 241 Marlborough; the poet Robert Lowell at 239.

➤Turn left on Fairfield a block to Beacon.

Fairfield is noted for its Queen Anne–style houses, characterized by color, animation, complicated and asymmetrical forms, detailing, and fine craftsmanship. Look for terra cotta, pressed-brick, wrought iron, and other design detailing here.

➤Turn right on Beacon five blocks to Arlington.

At 347 Beacon is another idiosyncratic Romanesque brick and brownstone by Besarick. An 1871 red brick house turned into a faux mini-chateau in 1907 by architect Ralph Adams Cram is at 334.

The building that saved Back Bay, a 1959 17-story high-rise so out of scale and character that it triggered height and other building restrictions, is at 330. At 266 is the first Renaissance-style building in Boston from 1886. Julia Ward Howe lived at 241. Now the Goethe Institute, 170 is Codman's 1900 design with an Adamesque facade and fancy interiors. An 1869 Victorian Gothic–style building is at 165. From 1882, 164 is covered with eye-catching geometric stonework and multicolored herringbone masonry. Emerson College's Abbott Library at 150 Beacon, once the Fuller Mansion, a 1904 Italian Renaissance Revival home, is open to the public; the library is on the site (but not the address—she assured that no one else would ever have that after she left) of the earlier home of Isabella Stewart Gardner. The Gibson House Museum and Victorian Society, New England Chapter, are at 137 in an 1860 building. Open to the public, they have intact middle-class nineteenth-century interiors and furnishings.

➤Turn right on Arlington and walk four blocks to Boylston (see Walk 1). Return three blocks down Boylston to the start.

➤At Arlington and Boylston, those using the T may enter Arlington T Stop, Green Line.

Walk 5

Waterfront

General location: Along Boston's downtown waterfront and continuing to Charlestown.

Special attractions: Boston Harbor, the Boston Tea Party Ship, the Computer/Children's Museums, World Trade Center, wharves and piers, New England Aquarium, Charlestown Bridge/Charlestown, *Old Ironsides*, Charlestown Navy Yard, and Bunker Hill Monument.

Difficulty rating: Generally easy; narrow, crowded streets, difficult crossings, and some hills.

Distance: 4 miles (unless using MBTA ferry).

Estimated time: 2 hours (unless using MBTA ferry).

Services: Restrooms and water are available at the World Trade Center, various museums and the aquarium,

Charlestown Navy Yard, and Bunker Hill Monument. Food and drink are available throughout.

Restrictions: None. The USS *Constitution*'s last tour begins (long lines are common) at 3:50 P.M.

For more information: Contact the Boston National Historic Park Visitor Center.

Getting started: Start at South Station at Atlantic Avenue and Summer Street. Drivers access this walk via I-93/Central Artery exit 22 to Summer and South Station. Uncovered commercial parking (wheelchair accessible) is available at Fan Pier by continuing on Atlantic to and right on Northern Avenue over Fort Point Channel and turning left onto Sleeper Street to Fan Pier parking on your right. Pedestrian garage access is from Sleeper. Pick up the walk at Northern.

Public transportation: Arrive at South Station T Stop, Red Line. Return from Community College T Stop, Orange Line, with a transfer to the Red Line at Downtown Crossing. Access to the Charlestown portion may be gained via MBTA ferry from Long Wharf. MBTA bus route 7 stops at South Station. MBTA route 92 goes from Charlestown's Main Street to Sullivan Square and Haymarket. MBTA ferries also leave from Charlestown Navy Yard to Long Wharf and Lovejoy Wharf (South Station).

Overview: See the New England Aquarium on the waterfront and *Old Ironsides* and Bunker Hill Monument in Charlestown—all "must sees"—plus wharves and piers, historic buildings, other ships and naval items, and fascinating museums.

Boston Harbor was the traditional source of Boston's prosperity and the site of many important historical

Waterfront

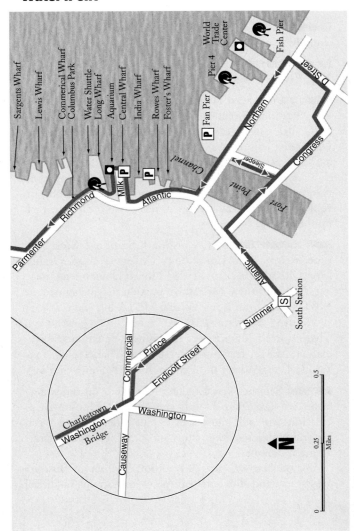

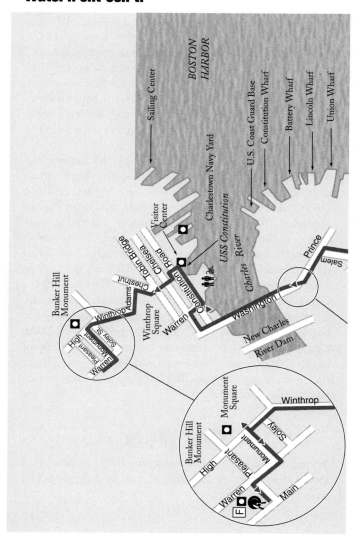

events. Although modified by dredging, landfill, and other human interventions, it remains large (41.21 square miles), sheltered, readily defensible, and commercially important. It is protected by two encircling arms of land, is filled with islands, and leads into Massachusetts Bay and from there into the North Atlantic Ocean. Boston in 1988 was said to have, and had fully earned recognition as having, the most polluted harbor in the United States. Implementation of a program to clean it up has been a great success. Boston Harbor is now a delight to those who live in, and who visit, Boston.

Charlestown, called "Mishawum" by the natives, was settled in 1629. The town and nearby river were named after King Charles. The settlers built a fort, laid out streets, and planned to receive the expected larger Puritan migration. When it came, Charlestown proved a poor choice. In the middle of a dry, hot summer, Charlestown's freshwater sources went dry. Many Puritans died. Most who survived accepted Blackstone's invitation to come to what is now central Boston. John Harvard was a Charlestownian. A sleepy rural town until the Revolution, Charlestown was burned nearly to the ground during the Battle of Bunker Hill. Largely rebuilt by 1800, Charlestown became a streetcar suburb and the home of largely "lace curtain" Irish—a middle-class step above their earthier countrymen. Boston annexed it in the mid-nineteenth century.

The Walk

►Start at South Station (built in 1899, renovated in 1989), cross Summer, and walk a block on Atlantic to and cross Congress.

You are on today's waterfront, not that of earlier times which extended much farther inland. The Federal Reserve Building to your right, with its missing fifth floor, is designed to reduce air downdrafts.

➤Turn right on Congress over Congress Street Bridge/Fort Point Channel.

This area is prime "Big Dig" territory (see page 16), so stay flexible!

➤Turn left along the channel.

You access three museums and the Boston Tea Party Ship here. The ship is in the channel under the bridge you just crossed and the Children's/Computer/Boston Fire Museums are side by side facing the channel on Museum Wharf and easily recognizable by the huge wooden milk bottle in front of the Children's Museum. The bottle is a former 1934 drive-in ice cream stand moved to this site in 1977 and again used as a snack stand.

The ship, *Beaver II,* is a re-creation of a ship—no original survives—loaded with tea chests which Patriots, ill-disguised as "Mohawk Indians," broke open and threw into the harbor on December 16, 1773. The Tea Party was actually held on what is now dry land about a block away and marked by a plaque at 470 Atlantic. The event's details are complex, but it had to do with British-imposed taxes. The matter and its consequences were serious. An American boycott of taxed British tea nearly bankrupted the East India Company. A special subsidy under the Tea Act was intended to bail out the company by giving special terms for American tea sales "consignees"—almost all the royal governor's cronies. In a popular, well-planned act, 342 chests weighing 360 pounds each—a total of 60 tons and worth millions in today's dollars—were destroyed. As punishment, Britain closed Boston Harbor to all boats, bringing economic disaster to Boston; abolished the colony's elected government; and required all trials be held in England. Visitors to the ship may relive that event by simulating throwing tea chests overboard, learning details of that night, and even seeing what is claimed to be an original jettisoned tea chest. Some of the actual tea is at the Old South Meeting Hall.

The Children's Museum is in a renovated warehouse and is an innovative pioneer in interactive exhibits for children. The Computer Museum was originally intended to display early, obsolete computer equipment as sort of a repository of historical curiosities. It is now very much a hands-on museum beloved by all children and most adults—and not just the family techno-nerd. The Boston Fire Museum is a place for all those who dreamed of becoming, or actually became, a fireman.

➤Return to Congress and turn left three blocks to D Street.

➤Turn left on D to Fish Pier.

Fish Pier is still the processor of much seafood for Boston but has been renovated for other commercial purposes. To your right and at a distance are the vast Boston Design Center—sales only to the trade—and the Black Falcon Cruise Terminal where large passenger vessels visiting Boston dock.

➤Turn left on Northern and stay right across Moakley Bridge to Atlantic.

You will pass on your right the World Trade Center, Anthony's Pier 4 restaurant on Pier 4, and the new Federal Courthouse on Fan Pier.

➤Turn right on Atlantic past Rowes Wharf, a handsome, modern building with many facilities and housing the

Water Shuttle Terminal, and India Wharf—1971 Harbor Towers by I. M. Pei, with apartments organized into pin-wheels rising 40 stories around a central core—to Milk Street.

➤Turn right on Milk onto Central Wharf and the New England Aquarium.

Bulfinch designed the original buildings on the wharf—completed in 1817. A fragment survives on the other side of the Central Artery. On the wharf is Susumu Shingu's 1983 steel and fiber-reinforced sculpture *Echo of the Waves*—known popularly as *The Whale*—which moves sinuously in response to subtle air currents.

See the aquarium at least once while in Boston! It was built in 1969 but has been repeatedly renovated and expanded since. At its center is a concrete box housing a three-story, 40-foot diameter tank filled with seawater and containing numerous large sea creatures and surrounded by a circular ramp that rises along the length of the tank. Illuminated tanks inset into the walls also contain sea life of various sorts. At the aquarium are seal pools and a floating arena for performing sea mammals. A former denizen was Hoover the Talking Seal—ask about him.

➤Continue along the waterfront a short distance to Long Wharf.

Long Wharf was constructed beginning in 1710. It was by far the biggest (1,800 feet) and most important of Boston's wharves. It continued to the foot of the Old State House. On it now are the 1981 Long Wharf Marriott Hotel with its distinctive silhouette on the waterfront skyline and the Chart House Restaurant in the 1763 Gardiner Building, once John Hancock's counting house.

➤Continue to adjacent Christopher Columbus Waterfront Park.

This is a 4.5-acre park created in 1976 by rerouting Atlantic Street and completion of the "walk to the sea" from City Hall. A cobblestone plaza is at the water's edge between the sea wall and promenade while elsewhere are playgrounds, flowers, trees, and benches.

Inland is a tall, obelisk-like building with a large clock face near its top. This is Marriott's Custom House at State and India Streets, a highly visible landmark. Built originally around 1840, on what was then the water's edge, as a four-faced Greek temple with fluted Doric columns and a skylit dome over the rotunda, today's great tower shot up through the roof of the existing building in 1914 to a height of 16 stories. This grossly exceeded Boston's building height restrictions—but as a federal building it was exempt from local rules! No longer a customs house, it is now a time-share apartment building with regularly scheduled tours.

Beyond you on the waterfront lie Commercial Wharf, Lewis Wharf, Sargents Wharf, Union Wharf, Lincoln Wharf, Battery Wharf, Constitution Wharf, and the U.S. Coast Guard Piers—the survivors of around 80 nineteenth-century wharves. They are now being rehabilitated, with warehouses being turned into condominiums, restaurants, and commercial space and new structures being built on renovated piers.

►Cross Atlantic from the park onto Richmond Avenue (becoming Parmenter) to walk across the North End (see Walk 3) and over the Charlestown Bridge or return to Long Wharf and take the MBTA ferry to Charlestown Navy Yard.

►If walking, stay right 0.3 mile to Salem Street.

►Turn right on Salem 0.1 mile to Prince Street.

➤Turn left on Prince 0.1 mile to Commercial Street.

➤Turn left a few feet on Commercial for access across the street to Charlestown Bridge (Washington Street).

➤Cross Commercial, enter the bridge-access ramp, and cross the bridge on the right.

From the bridge, you can see, among other things, Charlestown, Charlestown Navy Yard, *Old Ironsides*, the North End, Fleet Center (where the Celtics and the Bruins play) Bunker Hill Monument, and Bunker Hill. Mentioning these last two separately may surprise you. They are not the same! Bunker Hill is near a large gray church—St. Francis de Sales—to the left of Bunker Hill Monument. The monument is on Breed's Hill.

The crossing was once made by ferry—which the British closed as part of the "Intolerable Acts." The first Charlestown Bridge, a private venture, was opened in 1786; John Hancock was a stockholder. More than 1,500 feet long, it was the longest wooden bridge in the world. The current bridge was built in 1899.

The foot of the bridge in Charlestown is City Square—the place where the Puritans first settled in the Boston area. Puritans differed from "Pilgrims." Pilgrims were stricter, less prosperous and educated, and were in Holland for 12 years—their "pilgrimage"—before coming to America. Obstinate, intolerant, and sanctimonious, Puritans were also pious and moral, frugal and hard working, and devoted to learning and individual responsibility. Their congregationalist associations were classrooms in practical democracy. They faced great risk coming to a new land—many died in the early years. They settled and improved it and made it their home. Their presence is still felt in Boston after centuries and their descendants' decline into a tiny minority.

➤Turn right on the ramp leading from the bridge onto Chelsea Street, then right onto Warren Street. At the foot of Warren, cross and turn left onto Constitution Road to the Charlestown Navy Yard.

The Navy Yard Visitor Center/Bunker Hill Pavilion is the first building on the right. There you may use the facilities, obtain information, and watch the 30-minute multimedia reenactment of the Battle of Bunker Hill. In the immediate area are the USS *Constitution* (popularly known as *Old Ironsides*) and its museum, the USS *Cassin Young* World War II destroyer, and the buildings and grounds of the Charlestown Navy Yard itself.

The U.S. Navy was formed in 1793, and Charlestown Navy Yard was established in 1800 as the place where the Navy's ships were to be built, outfitted, and repaired. The first dry dock in the yard was built in 1840. The yard was closed in 1974, and the National Park Service acquired its western part for the Boston National Historical Park. Among the buildings at the yard is the Commandant's House, the yard chief's—he was also responsible for Boston Harbor's security—official residence. It was built in 1805. Lafayette and five U.S. presidents stayed here. It is open to visitors on summer weekends. Originally in Greek Revival style, as renovated the doubled-bowed facade and double conical roofs are patterned after Bulfinch's Federal style. The New England Museum Association occupies the basement. Also of interest at the yard are Dry Dock No. 1 (*Old Ironsides* was the first to enter it in 1833 and the last in it under Navy control in 1974); the ropewalk building where, for over a century, most of the Navy's rope was made; the Marine Barracks dating from 1810; the Boston Marine Society on First Avenue, since 1742 dedicated to making navigation safer, and

Bunker Hill Monument, *Charlestown.*

its museum of Boston maritime history; and Building 125 with an exhibit on the U.S. Navy's history (open on summer weekends).

The USS *Constitution* was launched in 1797, the U.S. Navy's third vessel. She is now the world's oldest commissioned warship afloat. Built at a North End shipyard across the river from her present berth, she is almost 300 feet long and about as tall as a 20-story building. Only around 20 percent of her timbers are original. She typically mounted 54 pieces of artillery and carried a crew of 450. Revere made her bolts and copper sheathing. Her popular name of *Old Ironsides* came from a crew member who, when he saw cannonballs bounce harmlessly off her 21-inch-thick live oak sides in her 1812 battle with the British frigate *Guerriere*, called her that. She saw battle in Tripoli against Algerian pirates in 1803 and in the War of 1812, when she sank two frigates and two sloops of the theretofore "invincible" British Navy. Never defeated and never boarded, she won 42 battles and captured 20 enemy vessels. When ironclads and steam power made her obsolete, she was almost broken up in 1830 but was saved by popular outcry in response to the poem in her defense written by the law student Oliver Wendell Holmes. Again in 1905, after she had long been demasted and used as a floating barracks, she avoided destruction due to public sentiment. She last sailed around the world in 1844–1845, was towed through the Panama Canal to visit U.S. Pacific ports in 1931–1934, but now only moves on July 4 when she is towed from dock and turned around. Last under full sail—36 sails and about an acre of canvas—in 1881, in 1997 she again felt the wind off Marblehead with a partial set of six sails. She is not expected to sail again. The USS *Constitution* Museum is in Building 22.

USS Constitution ("Old Ironsides"), *Charlestown Navy Yard.*

➤Exit the yard by Gate 1 onto Constitution for 150 feet and go through the pedestrian underpass on your right. Cross Chelsea, turn right, bear left to Chestnut Street, and go one block to Adams Street.

➤Turn left onto Adams and circle right as Adams borders Winthrop Square.

Winthrop Square, known as "Training Field" from 1632 when it was set aside for the militia, is surrounded by charming early-nineteenth-century buildings. In the square are memorial tablets containing the names of those who died at Bunker Hill.

➤Cross and turn right on Winthrop Street at the corner of Winthrop Square and stay left up Breed's Hill toward *Bunker Hill Monument* on Monument Square.

Monument Square is similarly surrounded with handsome buildings, these of the mid-nineteenth century.

The Battle of Bunker Hill and Bunker Hill Monument

The battle was named for Bunker Hill but was fought on Breed's Hill.

Britain needed to occupy Charlestown's high ground overlooking Boston and its harbor. Colonel William Prescott and 1,200 American troops got to Bunker Hill—Charlestown's tallest—first. Continuing to Breed's Hill, lower but nearer Boston, they fortified it. Major General William Howe's Redcoats landed on June 17, 1775, fired upon by colonial snipers, while another 1,300 to 2,800 Patriots arrived. Howe retaliated by torching deserted Charlestown. With 2,200 troops coming on line against them, if the Americans were *not* told "don't fire until you see the whites of their eyes," it would have been good advice due to then-current weaponry and tactics.

British first and immediate second assaults foundered. The Americans were short on ammunition and other supplies, had no reinforcements, and were patently not professional soldiers. A third assault prevailed. The battle lasted only two hours. Hundreds of patriots were lost. The survivors made an orderly retreat. British pursuit was half-hearted. Victory cost half the British troops. Britain never again moved from their Boston base. Howe became Britain's American commander, but Bunker Hill left him unnerved. Americans proved they could fight. They lost because of undiscipline, poor leadership, and insufficient provisions.

The 1843 *Bunker Hill Monument,* a granite obelisk 220 feet tall, was designed by Solomon Willard. At its base is a lodge with exhibits. Joseph Warren's 1857 statue is in the Park Service Building, and William Prescott's 1881 statue is on Monument Avenue. Construction took 21 years due to delays for insufficient funds. Lafayette laid its cornerstone in 1825. Daniel Webster was the orator at its 1843 dedication. It is owned and administered by the National Park Service. There are 294 difficult steps leading to a great view.

➤Turn left on High Street to a crossing point to Monument Square at Monument Avenue.

➤Cross the street, enter Monument Square, and tour *Bunker Hill Monument* and the grounds.

➤Depart Monument Square as you came and go down the hill on Monument Avenue a block across Warren Street.

➤Turn right on Warren a block to Pleasant Street.

➤Turn left on Pleasant a block to Main Street. This ends this walk.

On your right is the 1780 (renovated 1972) Warren Tavern at 2 Pleasant. Named for General Joseph Warren who died at Bunker Hill, it is now a restaurant. Washington refreshed himself here, and Paul Revere called it "my favorite place."

➤MBTA route 92 buses may be taken from Main Street to Haymarket, Boston. You may return to the Navy Yard for the MBTA ferry by turning left on Main. You may access Community College T Stop, Orange Line (a transfer at Downtown Crossing will return you to the start) by crossing Main, turning right three blocks to Austin Street, and turning left on Austin three blocks to the T stop on your right. If you are walking on Main toward town, there are two expensive but excellent restaurants (Olives and Figs) and the 1795 John Larkin House at No. 55–61. Mr. Larkin lent Paul Revere his horse.

Walk 6

Downtown

General location: Boston Center, Back Bay–Government Center.

Special attractions: Bay Village, Chinatown, shopping, old theaters, interesting architecture, and historic sites.

Difficulty rating: Easy; flat over generally good sidewalks.

Distance: 2 miles.

Estimated time: 1 hour.

Services: Restrooms and water are available at the State Street Visitor Center and at City Hall. Food and drink are available along the route.

Restrictions: None.

For more information: Contact State Street National Park Service Visitor Center.

Downtown

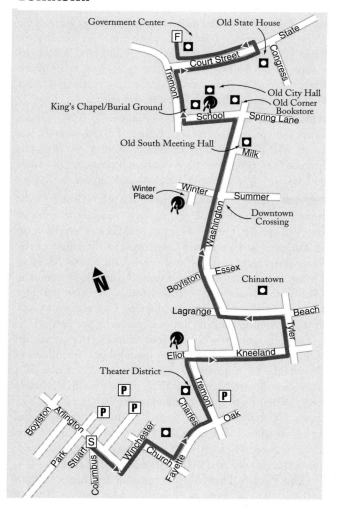

Getting started: Start at the Castle at Arlington and Stuart Streets. Drivers access this walk from I-90 exit 22 on Stuart to Arlington. Covered commercial parking (wheelchair accessible, clearance 6 feet) is available to your left at Park Plaza by continuing on Stuart past Arlington. Pedestrian garage is off Stuart. The parking garage exits on Park Plaza. Access to the start is gained by turning left on Park Plaza and walking a block to Arlington.

Public transportation: Arrive at Arlington T Stop, Green Line, and end at Government Center T Stop, Blue/Green Lines. MBTA bus route 9 stops at Arlington and Boylston Streets. Get to the start on Arlington by crossing Boylston and staying right for three blocks across Stuart.

Overview: This is "soup-to-nuts" essential Boston with something for everyone. From early nineteenth-century Bay Village, the Theater District, and Chinatown, pass on to shopping at Downtown Crossing and the edges of the Financial District, then finish with Old South Meeting House (now a museum), the Old Corner Bookstore, the Old State House (site of the Boston Massacre), King's Chapel and the Old Puritan Burying Ground, and Government Center with its famous "steaming tea kettle."

Bay Village is the old residential area generally within Arlington, Stuart, Charles, and Tremont Streets hidden in the middle of commercial downtown. Construction of a dam near Fayette Street in 1825 made building possible here. When Back Bay was filled in the 1860s, all Bay Village's 500 buildings were raised 12 to 18 feet to avoid being swamped. Edgar Allan Perry—his pen name was Poe—was born here in 1809 when his parents, both touring actors, stayed in a lodging house at 62 Carver.

The Theater District has been that for over a century and once had as many as 40 performance venues. It was a place of great and famous performances with opulent theaters, many of which remain and have been restored. Chinatown lies generally within Kneeland, Hudson, Essex, and Washington Streets. It was once a squalid neighborhood where the poorest of every sort lived. Only the Chinese stayed. Downtown Crossing is a place for great shopping, including famous Filene's Basement. King's Chapel and the Old Puritan Burial Ground are interesting places with interesting histories and graves of very interesting people. Everyone will want to visit the place where the Boston Massacre occurred. Government Center, the former site of the infamous Scollay Square, is now the location of Boston City Hall and other government buildings, many by noteworthy architects.

The Walk

➤Start facing the Castle at Arlington and Stuart.

The moated 1897 "Castle" (First Corps of Cadets Armory) was built by an old private militia as a virtual clubhouse. Some believe it was intended to repel attacks by the Irish on WASP Back Bay. It is now a convention and exhibition hall.

➤Go left on Arlington two blocks to Winchester Street's T Stop, cross Arlington, and go a block on Winchester to and cross Church Street. You are now in Bay Village.

The neighborhood was home to many speakeasies during Prohibition. Look around. Make diversions if something interests you.

➤Turn right on Church two blocks to Fayette.

➤Turn left on Fayette a block to and cross Charles.

Fayette—named for Lafayette—presents an attractive sampler of types of older buildings found in Bay Village.

The Old State House, Boston's Downtown.

➤Stay left a block as Fayette angles to the right and becomes Oak Street to Tremont.

➤Turn left on Tremont a block to Eliot/Stuart/Kneeland Street.

This is the Theater District. In the eighteenth century it was on the narrow neck of land—present-day Washington Street—linking Boston to the mainland and was lined with wharves.

Despite an unpropitious start—plays were banned until 1792—Boston has a glorious history of theater and entertainment. The first U.S. waltz was danced at Lorenzo Papanti's dance school. Jenny Lind sang here, Harry Houdini staged some of his most spectacular escapes here, and Boston was one of Charles Dickens's favorite stops on his American lecture tours. Vaudeville got its name at Keith's Theater, and burlesque started in Howard Athenaeum. Nonetheless, prudishness died hard. Boston performance licenses were regularly denied for failing to meet licensing office codes. Edward Albee in 1962 had to rewrite *Who's Afraid of Virginia Woolf* by removing all its profanity for its Boston performance. Boston was, since the 1920s, a place where plays were taken on the road for a shakedown—and often substantial revisions—before opening on Broadway. It also had an active theatrical life of its own. Boston's Theater District was once so dense with theaters that they were joined by underground passageways and lobbies to protect patrons moving among them in bad weather. There were 31 theaters in Boston in 1900 with a total of 50,000 seats. Nickelodeons and their successors, motion pictures, doomed large-scale live theatrical entertainments, and many of Boston's theaters were converted into movie houses. D. W. Griffith's *Birth of a Nation* premiered in Boston in 1915. Today, Boston has performances of and venues for entertainment of every imaginable sort, from symphonies and orchestras, opera and ballet companies, and professional dramatic performances to popular and ethnic musicians, amateur performers and performances, and street buskers (entertainers) almost everywhere. Buskers are often very good. Some now-famous entertainers got their professional starts by performing on the streets of Boston and Cambridge. Berklee School of Music and Emerson College, among others, offer excellent theatrical and performance education.

The 1909 Schubert Theatre at 265 Tremont on your left was a principal site for many famous shows on their pre-Broadway tryouts. *Away We Go* came here for tryouts in 1943. After rewrites, it left town as *Oklahoma!*

Across the street at 268 is the 1924 Wang Center/Music Hall. Originally the Metropolitan Theater, it was built in 1932 as a lavishly decorated movie palace with an Art Deco restaurant, the Platinum Salon. Modeled on the Paris Opera House, its Grand Lobby was based on Versailles Palace. It had its own staffed medical station for emergencies. It could accommodate 4,000 people at each of its four daily showings. Famous entertainers often appeared in person prior to a film showing. It was renovated, expanded, and renamed in 1982 at a cost of $10 million. It is now a principal stage for quality productions.

The 1914 Wilbur Theatre at 246 is basically in Colonial Revival style. It was the site for premieres of Thornton Wilder's *Our Town* and Tennessee Williams's *Streetcar Named Desire* with Marlon Brando and Jessica Tandy. A cafe operates from the lower lobby.

Before leaving Tremont, look down Stuart. On your

left at a distance is the 1902 Emerson Majestic Theatre at 219—known for musicals and light opera and restored by Emerson College. Beyond is the Colonial Theatre (see Walk 1).

►Turn right on Kneeland three blocks to Tyler Street.

Jacob Wirth Restaurant at the corner of Stuart and Tremont is a great place to eat for those not wishing to try the delicious foods from all over East Asia available in Chinatown.

"Chinatown" is a misnomer. Many Asian people and businesses within Chinatown are not Chinese. Chinatown has outgrown its designated confines. Chinese ethnics live and operate businesses throughout the Boston area. Non-Asians live, and non-Asian businesses operate, within Chinatown. The Chinese gate entrance and the pagoda phone booths are for tourists. Nevertheless, Chinatown has been and remains the cultural center for many Boston-area East Asian and Chinese ethnics. Its shops and restaurants attract them, as they do non-Asians and out-of-town visitors. Chinese first came to Boston in the eighteenth century as a consequence of the Boston–Far East maritime trade. Nineteenth-century Boston was vitally dependent on China trade and prospered in large part because of the special friendship that Chinese merchant Houqua had for Americans when all Chinese foreign trade was handled through Canton. Substantial Asian immigration started in the 1870s when 200 Chinese imported as strikebreakers in Lawrence gravitated to Boston once the strike was broken. These were joined by transcontinental railroad Chinese laborers when that project was finished. By 1931, Chinatown had about 1,200 residents. It grew rapidly thereafter. Vietnamese, Cambodians, and Thais, among others, followed the Chinese. A tong (Chinese gang) war left four dead and many others wounded after a 1926 ambush on Oxford Place—an alley running between Oxford Street and Harrison Avenue. Sun Yat-Sen and Ho Chi Minh walked these streets when their names were unknown.

➤Turn left on Tyler and go a block to Beach Street.

Dr. Sun Yat-Sen came to the United States in 1905. He arrived in Boston, found seven men willing to work with him, and began from the basement of 12 Tyler his organization of the overthrow of the Ching Dynasty. He was successful. He established the Chinese Republic in 1911.

The poet/philosopher Kahlil Gibran lived on Tyler. At Beach is the large Chinese gate, a gift from Taiwan, which is the official entrance to Chinatown.

➤Turn left on Beach and go two blocks to and cross Washington.

➤Turn right on Washington 0.4 mile to School Street.

Washington—its name was changed in 1789 to honor George Washington's Boston visit—is the old thoroughfare linking the Old State House with the town gate at the end of the neck of the Shawmut Peninsula.

On Washington between Essex and Kneeland Streets is the so-called Combat Zone—since the 1960s, Boston's officially designated adult entertainment district. It hangs on by merely a G-string now. Rough bars, girlie reviews, and the like were theoretically confined here. Most are gone. The wages of sin may be death, but down-market sins' monetary wages cannot pay Boston's high downtown rents!

Boston is known for prudery. The Puritans were famous for rigorous enforcement of moral rules. The Watch and Ward Society started protecting public morality in 1878. The ACLU got Boston to stop censorship in 1965—but *Hair* was closed for four weeks in 1970 for desecrating the flag. "Banned in Boston" was once a common phrase. Condemnation by Boston's League of Decency could make a book or motion picture a hit elsewhere. Boston also has a reputation for vice. Around 1770, northwest Beacon Hill was called "Mount Whoredom." It was only cleaned up in 1823 by raids led by Mayor Josiah Quincy. Scollay Square was a rough, waterfront neighborhood that sailors and others regularly visited for vices practiced commercially there. When razed, government offices replaced bars and gambling dens. The effect on the level of vice is unclear.

At the intersection of Washington and Boylston, look down Boylston to your left. No. 2–22 Boylston is the China Trade Center. At 48 Boylston is the 1875 Young Men's Christian Union, among Boston's few remaining Ruskin Gothic–style buildings. At the corner of Washington and Essex Streets is the former site of the Liberty Tree, indicated by a marker in the pavement. It was planted in 1646. The Sons of Liberty regularly met under it before the Revolution to object to British colonial practices.

The 1876 building at 523 Washington houses the 1913 Modern Theatre, one of Boston's first movie theaters and the first anywhere that was acoustically designed. *The Jazz Singer,* the first talking film, premiered here in the late 1920s.

The 1928 Savoy Theatre—originally the B. F. Keith Memorial Theatre and named for the man who introduced the term "vaudeville" and the owner of over 400 theaters—at 539 Washington has a flamboyant Spanish Baroque facade and lavish (to garish) interiors. The 1931

Paramount Theatre at 549 Washington is Boston's most stylish, both inside and out, old Art Deco movie house.

Washington Street Mall/Downtown Crossing is a pedestrian mall that runs along Washington Street from Temple Place to Milk Street in an area completely devastated by the 1872 fire. Downtown Crossing is well known for its vibrant atmosphere, its street musicians, its pedestrian-friendly brick streets, its many vendors selling from pushcarts with their brightly colored awnings, and its mixture of historical and architectural sights, hotels and restaurants, the largest jewelry district in New England, specialty shops and districts, and many businesses selling merchandise and services. You are now at the center of Boston's famed shopping district. On the corner of Summer at 426 Washington is the 1912 Filene's. Beyond Filene's at 26–38 Summer is the interesting architectural preservationist compromise of integrating the 1874 Kennedys dry goods and clothing store into the 1989 101 Arch Street building—itself quite interesting with its Deco Revival motifs, giant clock, and postmodern pediment on its skyline. Across from Filene's on Summer is its competitor, once Jordan Marsh but now Macy's, in a largely 1950s International style.

Whole Boston streets once specialized in gloves, pianos, etc. Boston is still a great place to shop for specialty purchases, such as used and new books. Eben Dyer Jordan came to Boston from Danville, Maine, with $1.25 to his name, started business at 168 Hanover in the North End, and went on to found (with Benjamin L. Marsh) the Jordan Marsh department store chain in 1851. A few years later, Roland H. Macy of Nantucket opened *his* store on Hanover, the first predecessor store of R. H. Macy Company. Macy's now operates Jordan Marsh stores under its own name. Under Filene's store is Filene's Basement, the pioneer since 1908 of the automatic markdown, by which each item is tagged with the date of arrival and a sale price. That price is automatically discounted by a certain percentage based on the elapsed time from its date of arrival. Shoppers' visits here are part bargain hunting, part historical pilgrimage, and—when a big sale is on—part fascinating sociological phenomenon.

On Hamilton Place to your left and visible across Washington from Filene's is the 1852 (repeatedly altered) Orpheum Theater (formerly the Old Music Hall). The New England Conservatory began here, and the Boston Symphony Orchestra played its first performance here in 1881. It was the site of the world premiere of the Tchaikovsky First Piano Concerto and the American premiere of the Second Symphony by Brahms. It is once again a performance theater.

The 1729 Old South Meeting Hall is at Washington and Milk Streets. This Christopher Wren–influenced building, with its handsome wooden spire atop a balustraded brick tower, is Boston's second oldest church. It is on the site of John Winthrop's garden and of a 1670 wooden church where Benjamin Franklin was baptized in 1705. Town meetings leading to the Boston Tea Party were held here. It was heavily damaged by occupying British troops, came within a whisker of being burned in the 1872 fire, and escaped—through a successful public appeal for funding for its preservation—razing for commercial development in 1876. It has been operated as a museum and monument by the Old South Association since then.

Franklin's birthplace at 17 Milk is now the site of the 1875 Boston Post Building. Recognition of Franklin's birth there was incorporated into the building's cast-iron—resembling stone—facade.

On your right lies Boston's Financial District and economic core.

The 1718 Old Corner Bookstore (formerly the Thomas Crease House and the site of exiled, excommunicated Anne Hutchinson's house) is at 285 Washington. First an apothecary shop with living space for the owner, it became associated with publishing in 1828 when a young publisher renovated the house. It has remained so ever since. It was the offices of Ticknor and Fields (publishers of Longfellow, Lowell, Whittier, Hawthorne, Holmes, Thoreau, Emerson, Tennyson, Browning, Thackeray, Dickens, and Harriet Beecher Stowe as well as *The Atlantic Monthly* magazine) and was the regular meeting place for the Boston, Cambridge, and Concord literati when these were America's unquestioned intellectual and cultural leaders. The *Boston Globe* bought it and converted it into the present travel bookstore.

►Turn left on School three blocks to Tremont.

On your right before turning is Spring Lane, the site of a freshwater spring that once supplied water for early Boston. It is bordered by the 1893 Winthrop Building at 276–278 Washington, with its unusual curving form dictated by neighboring streets' paths.

The 1863 Old City Hall at 45 School is on the site of the Boston Public Latin School of 1635, America's first public school, which gave the street its name. Old City Hall is in an elaborate French Second Empire–style building dominated by a florid central pavilion. Attractive, ornate interiors were removed when the building was renovated for modern offices and a restaurant—Maison Robert—in 1970. In front are statues of Benjamin Franklin, born a Bostonian, and Josiah Quincy.

To your left on Tremont is the Parker House Hotel (see Walk 1).

➤ Turn right on Tremont a block to Court Street.

King's Chapel and Old Puritan Burying Ground are at 58 Tremont.

King's Chapel—called Stone Chapel immediately after the Revolution—was built in 1749 to serve a congregation formed by British officers in 1686. The earlier wooden structure for the congregation was built without authorization on the grounds of the Puritan Burying Ground when Boston's Puritan leaders refused to sell any land for the construction of a hated Anglican church. The dead earliest Puritan leaders must have rested uneasily lying next to the services of their sectarian foes. To not disrupt services and to deter any effort to prevent the building of the new church once the old had been torn down, the new building was constructed around the outside of the old wooden building, then the old building was dismantled and removed and the new church's interior was installed. The walls are of granite 4 feet thick, so the congregation must have felt some continuing hostility. Designed by Peter Harrison, the present church is a fine example of American Georgian architecture. A planned elaborate steeple was not built because of lack of funds. The wood colonnade of Ionic columns, by the same architect, was added in 1786. The interior is divided into pews owned or rented by families. One pew was reserved for important personages, such as royal governors and President Washington. Slaves sat in the rear in a gallery near the cemetery. Condemned prisoners had a special pew to the right of the main entrance, where they were forced to listen to a sermon before being hanged on the Common. With the departure of many Anglican Tory parishioners after the Siege of Boston, the church became—in 1789—America's first Unitarian church.

The Puritan Burying Ground, from 1631, is Boston's oldest. Early governors John Winthrop and John Endicott; Elizabeth Paine, model for Hester Prynne; William Dawes, who rode with Paul Revere that fateful night; and the cleric John Cotton are among those buried here.

➤Turn right on Court 0.2 mile to the Old State House.

The original Boston settlement was near here at Town Cove, about the intersection of State and Congress Streets.

The Boston Massacre took place in King Street at the base of the Old State House. Young rowdies, egged on by demagoguery, were looking for trouble and found it. They pelted British sentries with stones and snowballs and threatened to kill the soldiers. The confrontation got out of hand. British soldiers fired in fear of their lives. Five Americans lay dead on March 5, 1770. Paul Revere did much to make the Boston Massacre famous and a rallying point for opposition to the British with his lurid, inaccurate engraving of the event. The spot where the "martyrs" fell is marked with a circle of paving stones.

At the head of Washington (leading across the neck to Roxbury and beyond) and State (leading to Long Wharf and the heart of Boston's commerce), the Old State House was at the center of much important early Boston history. It replaced a wooden 1657 Town House that burned in 1711. The Old State House (the Second Town House, as it was known) was built in 1713. It included rooms for the provincial governor, the courts, the House of Representatives, the Suffolk Register of Deeds, and a ground floor merchants' exchange. A 1747 fire devastated the building's interior. Although the center of British colonial government, the Old State House was also the place where Sam Adams and the legislature resolved that there should be no taxation without representation. Boston's first public reading of the Declaration of Independence was from its second-floor balcony. Soon thereafter, Patriot mobs took the lion and unicorn—symbols of British authority—from the building and burned them. Those here now are reproductions. Boston acquired the building in the 1790s. It burned again in 1830. It was vacated in the 1860s. Boston attempted unsuccessfully, through atrocious renovations, to interest buyers in it. By 1876, the building was generally abandoned and a hoarding for billboards. Chicago offered to move it there, which spurred Boston to reconsider. Restored in 1881, it was leased to the Bostonian Society, which has maintained a museum in it since. The first floor has a permanent exhibition on Boston's Revolutionary history. Temporary exhibitions are on the second floor.

➤Cross and turn left on Court until you can walk onto the plaza to your right. Go in. This is Government Center.

The charming, curving, Federal-style 1816 Sears Crescent commercial block and its small granite neighbor, the 1848 Sears Block, have been saved but stranded on City Hall Plaza.

The most distinctive—and a local sentimental favorite—thing to see here is the famous steaming tea kettle that hangs above a shop, long the Oriental Tea Company but now a Starbucks coffee house. When it was new in 1873, a prize was offered for the person who could guess nearest the kettle's capacity. When time came to judge the guesses, with 15,000 people assembled, the lid was removed and one boy after another came out—eight in all—followed by a man in a tall silk hat. The correct amount was 227 gallons, 2 quarts, 1 pint, and 3 gills, but one paper editor said he had guessed "300 gals" and was surprised to find it held only "8 boys."

Alexander Graham Bell first transmitted the human voice by wire in 1875 in Scollay Square. The actual attic room where he invented the telephone is preserved in 185 Franklin Street.

Amid Boston's blot of Harvard crimson, there is a redeeming spot of Yale blue! Elihu Yale was born around here in 1649.

The 56-acre Government Center was developed under a 1960 master plan by I. M. Pei and Partners, replacing notorious Scollay Square. The massive 1965 Boston City Hall sits on a vast plaza. Its top-heavy mass and overhanging sun screens are said to be reminiscent of LeCorbusier's convent at La Tourette and the ancient Mexican Zapotec city of Monte Alban. Also part of Government Center are the 1896 Suffolk County Court House and the John F. Kennedy Federal Office Building, the design of Walter Gropius.

➤This ends the walk. Return to Arlington T Stop near the start via the clearly visible Government Center T Stop, Blue/Green Lines.

Walk 7

Logan Airport/East Boston

General location: East Boston near Logan Airport.

Special attractions: Views of Boston Harbor and its shore-line, a lovely park on a pier, and a major U.S. immigrant historical entry point.

Difficulty rating: Easy; somewhat lengthy, but generally flat and well paved with avoidable stairs.

Distance: 2.75 miles.

Estimated time: 1.5 hour.

Services: Restrooms and water are available at Piers Park, Harbor Ferry Terminal, and the Harborside Hyatt Hotel. Food and drink are available at the Harborside

Logan Airport/East Boston

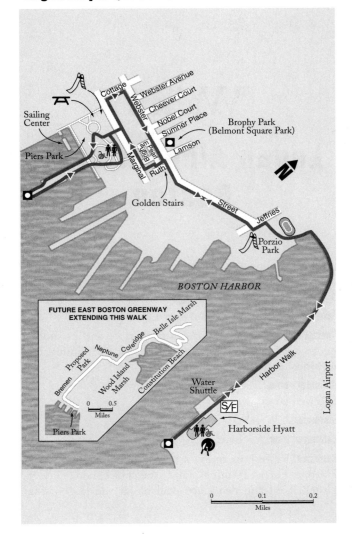

Sailing Center

Piers Park

Cottage

Webster

Marginal

Webster Avenue

Cheever Court

Nobel Court

Sumner Place

Lamson

Brophy Park
(Belmont Square Park)

Bright

Pearl

Ruth

Golden Stairs

Street

Jeffries

Porzio Park

BOSTON HARBOR

**FUTURE EAST BOSTON GREENWAY
EXTENDING THIS WALK**

Proposed Park

Neptune

Coleridge

Belle Isle Marsh

Constitution Beach

Bremen

Wood Island Marsh

Piers Park

0   0.5
Miles

Water Shuttle

Harbor Walk

Logan Airport

S/F

Harborside Hyatt

0   0.1   0.2
Miles

Hyatt Hotel, airport terminals, and nearby East Boston restaurants.

Restrictions: None. The walking impaired may reverse the Piers Park return route and avoid the Golden Stairs. The route is safe. Much is constantly patrolled.

For more information: Contact MassPort for information on transportation alternatives to and from the airport and Piers Park.

Getting started: Start at Harbor Ferry Terminal. Drivers access this walk via the Callahan/Sumner Tunnel or the Tobin Bridge and follow signage to Logan Airport. Park near airport terminals. Go to the start as instructed below.

Public transportation: Get to the airport by (a) water shuttle or water taxi; (b) MBTA buses and special Logan Expresses from Braintree and Framingham; or (c) subway to the Airport T Stop, Blue Line. At the airport, take a free special Harbor Ferry Terminal Number 66 shuttle bus—running regularly—from the Airport T Stop, any terminal, or the Logan Office Center—identifiable by a life buoy on its front and "Water Transportation" on its sides.

Overview: This walk is for those stuck at Logan Airport or anyone wanting great views of Boston Harbor or a better acquaintance with East Boston. Walk by the water along lovely Harbor Walk through an interesting, historic part of East Boston to Piers Park—aptly named since it is a charming park on a renovated pier.

East Boston—"Eastie" to locals—was settled by Europeans before Boston. It was, at least at low tide, originally five islands. Noddle Island was, in 1637, the first neighborhood annexed by Boston. Landfill joined all five islands into one around 1830. Noddle and Breed/Hog Islands are East Boston's residential and commercial area.

Noddle Island Pavilion, Piers Park, East Boston.

Logan Airport covers the remaining two-thirds—Governor's, Apple, and Bird Islands—and Wood Island Park, once one of Olmsted's handsomest parks. East Boston is now attached to the mainland but not to Boston. It was long used for farming, grazing, and military fortifications and lightly settled, and an early, important Revolutionary War battle—Chelsea Creek—was fought here. East Boston's history is rooted in shipping, manufacturing, and transportation. It was where many famous clipper sailing ships—most notably those of the premier builder of such ships, Donald McKay—were built, where many ships entering and leaving Boston Harbor berthed, and where most immigrants coming to Boston first set foot on their new American home. Although promoted in the 1830s as a salubrious, cool seaside retreat when noted persons settled here and built grand houses, its social cachet did not last. It became a favored home for recently arrived immigrant ethnic communities. Although thought of as an Italian ethnic area, recent changes have added Hispanics, Asians, and others.

The Walk

➤From Harbor Ferry Terminal—a small, 12-sided building where water passengers purchase tickets and wait out of the weather—go to the concrete path along the water.

Above the interior windowed walls of the terminal, Mela Lyman created a 74-foot-long homage to water through a frieze of paintings depicting swimmers.

➤Turn left. The descending steps lead to water transportation. The Harborside Hyatt Hotel and Logan Airport are to your left. You are on Harbor Walk.

Logan Airport is over 2 miles from Boston center and separated from Boston by the harbor. Tunnel traffic jams make it seem farther. Massachusetts Port Authority (MassPort) operates it. It was named for General Edward Lawrence Logan, Boston city councilman, legislator, judge, and a military officer during the Spanish-American War and World War I and in the National Guard. His 1956 bronze statue—larger than life—by Joseph A. Coletti is at the airport entrance mall. The airport was built in 1923 as Boston Municipal Airport, was rebuilt and renamed Boston International Airport in 1947, and has been repeatedly expanded. It is still being renovated. It has five terminals, designated "A" through "E," and covers two-thirds of East Boston.

➤Go 300 yards to Harbor Walk's end.

Boston Harbor is to your immediate right, and Boston's shoreline and skyline are in the distance. Note the walk's statuary. The monument at walk's end has, etched into its interior stone wall surface, the names and locations of things seen on the horizon. An enumeration of the piers and some other things you see on the Boston waterfront across the harbor are found in Walk 5.

There are public boat trips offered for whale watching, fishing, or just being out on a cruise. There are more than 30 islands in Boston Harbor—some actually in Massachusetts Bay. They range from less than an acre to 214 acres and comprise 1,200 land acres all together. They are scattered over 50 square miles of water. No other American city has so many islands so near.

➤Reverse your route and continue 0.5 mile to Porzio Park.

Note in passing Carlos Dorrien's 1985 *Portal and Stelle,* four pieces of stone 6.5 to 14 feet high, and William Wainright's 1982 *Windwheels*—stainless steel with diffraction grating, 16 to 20 feet in height—which varies in prismatic color as kinetic parts move in the wind.

➤At the end of Harbor Walk, turn right and enter Porzio Park.

The park was named for Joseph Porzio, an artist and East Boston community leader commemorated by a plaque at the park's entrance. The park has playground areas for children, picnic benches, public tennis courts, and other children's amusement and adult exercise equipment. Facilities are being modernized and expanded.

➤Cross the park 0.5 mile to Jeffries Street.

➤Turn left on Jeffries 100 feet to and cross Webster Street.

This is Jeffries Point. To your left down Jeffries at the intersection of Webster is Jeffries Yacht Club, the oldest chartered U.S. yacht club.

➤Turn right on Webster, stay left, and go 0.25 mile up the hill to Lamson Street.

Handsome early-nineteenth-century homes stand along what is called Captains' Row—named in the belief that early residents were ships' captains.

To your left is a grassy easement where a narrow gauge railway once climbed from the wharves and shipyards to carry passengers and freight to East Boston, Revere, and Lynn. The trains and much of the ship traffic are gone, but the shipyards remain. You can see their cranes and buildings on the shore to your left. A capped tunnel through which the train ran lies beneath the easement.

On your right front is the 1833 Belmont Square Park. British troops were stationed and trained here—when it was known as Camp Hill—from 1697 to 1711. They were still being trained here when they evacuated Boston in 1776. American troops encamped here in 1812.

➤At Lamson, turn left a block down an asphalt incline officially known—at least in its upper reaches—as Ruth Street but locally referred to as the Golden Stairs. Walking impaired continue on Webster to Cottage, turn left to Marginal Street, and resume the walk at the marked Piers Park entrance.

Until the 1950s, most foreign immigrants to Boston cleared immigration at buildings below these stairs and then are believed to have begun their lives in their new land by walking up this incline. Boston was the second largest immigration point on the East Coast. One immigration building remains. It is to the left at the edge of the fenced-in shipyard. To the right as you descend the stairs is a tiny public park—designated an "urban wild" and maintained by the Boston Parks Department—with great views of Boston Harbor.

▶At the bottom, turn right and walk 150 feet on Marginal.

To your right and up the hill is the rear of the Samuel Adams Public Elementary School—site of John F. Kennedy's father, Joseph's, boyhood home. "Joe" was born nearby.

▶Turn left, cross Marginal, and enter the marked gates of Piers Park.

In 1995, MassPort built Piers Park at a cost of $17 million. It is 6.5 acres and built on an old, abandoned, but now refurbished 600-foot pier and immediately adjacent land. An adjoining pier will later be reconditioned and added to the park for a total of 12 acres. Construction of a greenway has begun that will join Piers Park by 3.5 miles of green areas and urban walking routes with Wood Island Marsh; Constitution Beach, a public bathing beach; and Belle Isle Marsh, a large saltwater marsh and nature preserve. At the administrative building is an office for the bicycle-mounted police who patrol the park around the clock.

The pier is filled with benches and labeled trees. Part of the park and adjoining the pier is the Piers Park Sailing Center. Boston-area visitors are unlikely to have time to demonstrate sailing skills to qualify for boat rentals, but you may take a three-hour introductory course of sailing instruction on these boats at an individual hourly fee—each boat accommodates up to five trainees. Instruction may include travel to some Boston Harbor islands by special prior arrangement.

➤Walk Piers Park's grounds.

There are two open pavilions; a modern children's playground, complete with much interesting playground equipment, including a playing fountain that is a hit with kids on hot days; picnic tables; an outdoor adult fitness station; green space for playing fields; a small amphitheater (performances regularly on Sunday evenings and irregularly at other times); an administrative building with public restrooms; a sailing school marina; and brick strolling pathways.

The first pavilion is faced with William Reimann's series of carved granite panels. Each has images reflecting a different present or historical East Boston immigrant group. Rubbings may be made. A guide to each panel is inside the pavilion. Each pavilion section is named for a different East Boston neighborhood. In front of this pavilion and embedded in the pavement is Reimann's carved granite disc with "images of East Boston." At the end of the pier is a second pavilion named in honor of Donald McKay, famous builder of clipper ships on East Boston's waterfront. This pavilion has a centrally lighted column and wonderful views of Boston and Boston Harbor.

The abandoned pier to your right will be converted for the next extension to the park.

➤Leave as you entered and cross Marginal.

➤Turn left, then right onto and ascend Cottage 0.05 mile to Webster Street.

Note the Victorian-era houses painted in bright colors. Granite curbs line the street. At Webster, look left and across the street to the plaque high on the side of a house commemorating the site of East Boston's first house.

➤Turn right past Belmont Square Park and retrace your path 0.95 mile to the start.

Walk 8

The Fens

General location: South of Back Bay on the Emerald Necklace.

Special attractions: Fenway Park, the Boston Museum of Fine Arts, the Isabella Stewart Gardner Museum, and a walk among greenery.

Difficulty rating: Easy; flat terrain over good sidewalks.

Distance: 2.5 miles.

Estimated time: 1.25 hours.

Services: Restrooms and water are available at Fenway Park and the museums. Food and drink are available at museum cafeterias.

Restrictions: None.

For more information: Contact Fenway Park, Isabella Stewart Gardner Museum, and Boston Museum of Fine Arts.

The Fens

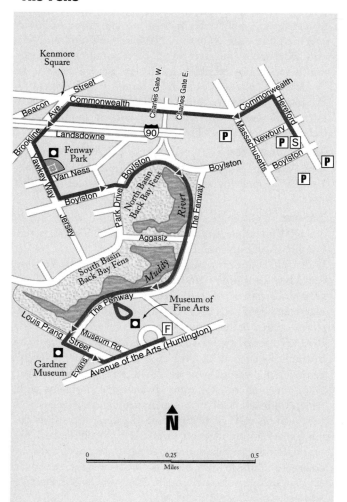

Kenmore Square

Beacon Street

Brookline Ave.

Commonwealth

Charles Gate W.

Charles Gate E.

Commonwealth

Hereford

Landsdowne

90

Massachusetts

Newbury

P

P S

Yawkey Way

Fenway Park

Van Ness

Boylston

Boylston

Boylston

P

P

Jersey

Park Drive

Boylston

North Basin
Back Bay Fens

River

The Fenway

Aggasiz

South Basin
Back Bay Fens

Muddy

The Fenway

Museum of
Fine Arts

Louis Prang

The Fenway

Museum Rd.

F

Gardner
Museum

Evans

Street

Avenue of the Arts (Huntington)

N

0   0.25   0.5
Miles

Getting started: Start at the Institute for Contemporary Art. Drivers access this walk from I-90 by exit 21, otherwise from I-93/Central Artery by exit 26 onto Storrow Drive and then left, onto Massachusetts Avenue south, and left onto Boylston to the start on your left. Commercial parking (wheelchair accessible, clearance 6 feet) is available at Prudential Center, accessed by continuing on Boylston to Prudential Center on your right. Pedestrian garage access is from Boylston. Cross and turn left on Boylston and walk two blocks across Hereford Street to the start.

Public transportation: Start at Hynes/ICA T Stop and return from Museum of Arts T Stop, Green Line. MBTA routes 1 and 55 stop at Hynes Center across the street from the start.

Overview: Y'gotta see Fenway once before they tear it down! While there, get a little culture at the Fine Arts and Gardner Museums amid gentle greenery.

A "fen" is a marshy region. That describes the Fens or Back Bay Fens when landscape architect Frederick Law Olmsted began work on it in 1879. The Fens was once salt marsh and reed beds because of the uncontrolled tidal and storm surges of the saline Charles River. Sewage from Roxbury carried typhoid and created a stench. Olmsted's hydraulics solved these problems while creating a lovely, landscaped pleasure park of 78.58 acres. Charles River Dam and modern sanitation obviated the problems with which Olmsted dealt. Subsequent vegetation changes and the addition of Victory and Rose Gardens and sports facilities never intended by Olmsted have obliterated his original concept. Surrounding the park are over a dozen colleges and universities, baseball's Fenway Park, two great art museums, handsome residences, several large hospitals, and venerable Boston institutions.

Fenway Park, a rare relic of old-style professional baseball fields, opened in 1912 the week the *Titanic* sank; it was rebuilt in 1934. Seating capacity is 33,871, but standing-room seats are also sold. Its most famous feature is the so-called Green Monster, a wall standing 37 feet tall in left field. The Green Monster originally compensated for nearby railroad tracks that prevented extension of the park's left field. Its height is said to reflect the owner's miserliness. He did not want the expense of baseballs lost over a lower wall. The red seat in the bleachers is where Ted Williams's longest-hit home run landed.

The Walk

➤Start at the Institute of Contemporary Art at 941–955 Boylston in a renovated 1886 police station. Face Hereford, turn left, and go two blocks to Commonwealth Avenue.

➤Turn left and stay left 0.6 mile to Kenmore Square.

Pass Charles Gate, crossing Stony Brook, which drains the Fens, Muddy River, and other water sources above it and empties into the Charles River. Kenmore Square is identifiable by the nearby Citgo sign, a beloved Boston landmark and a ready locator for Fenway Park. Kenmore Square is Boston University territory. BU and its denizens largely fill the area from Kenmore Square south for some distance along the east bank of the Charles.

➤Turn left on Brookline Avenue and stay left 0.15 mile to Yawkey Way.

➤Turn left on Yawkey and stay left 0.1 mile to Fenway Park.

Fenway Park is a professional major league baseball stadium where the Boston Red Sox play.

The Boston Braves played World Series home games here in 1914 while their own field was under construction. Professional and college football games were also played here. The Red Sox last won the World Series in 1918. In 1920, the Red Sox sold Babe Ruth to the New York Yankees. This—the "Curse of the Bambino"—is said to be the reason why no Red Sox team has ever won the World Series since—or "until this year," as Red Sox fans invariably say.

On the Kenmore Square side on Landsdowne Street are some of Boston's most popular late-night dance establishments.

➤Leave Fenway Park and continue left along Yawkey 0.1 mile to Boylston.

➤Turn left on Boylston for 0.35 mile and cross Boylston as it enters Back Bay Fens Park and crosses over Stony Brook by H. H. Richardson's Boylston Street Bridge.

➤Leave Boylston as it goes to the left and continue on the bend to the right of, and stay right on, The Fenway 0.6 mile to the Museum of Fine Arts. Walk into the Fens at any time to continue your walk on a parallel path or to embark on new discoveries.

On your left at a distance is the 1901 Berklee College of Music at 1140 Boylston in a particularly frenetic Georgian style; the Massachusetts Historical Society—America's oldest historical society dating from 1791—at 1154 Boylston in an 1899 Georgian Revival brick double bowfront; and the Boston Conservatory of Music at 8 Fenway. Victory Gardens—dating from World War II—are in the park on the other side of the North Basin.

In the Fens are a Japanese temple bell of 1675 given by Japan as a symbol of world peace, a 1937 stone statue of early Puritan leader John Endicott, and Daniel Chester

Appeal to the Great Spirit *statue in front of the Boston Museum of Fine Arts, the Fens.*

French's 1896 bronze-and-stone statue of the Irish-born, historically interesting John Boyle O'Reilly.

Farther on your left is Northeastern University. The Boston University Theater at 264 Huntington Avenue and the New England Conservatory of Music and Jordan Hall at Nos. 290–294 are of interest. The conservatory was, in 1867, the first American music college while Jordan Hall has some of the best acoustics and some of the oddest seating of any performance hall. The James P. Kelleher Rose Garden to your right across the South Basin is a large, excellent rose garden worth visiting in season. To your left is the Boston Museum of Fine Arts.

➤Enter the Art Museum, housed in a massive granite 1908 Classical Revival building with two flanking wings—the West Wing was designed by I. M. Pei—at 465 Huntington. The rear view of the building from The Fenway, with a long, two-story Ionic colonnade along a flat facade, is attractive. In front is Cyrus E. Dallin's 1908 bronze *Appeal to the Great Spirit*. Founded in 1876 and one of the largest U.S. art museums, the Art Museum has more than 1,000,000 objects in its permanent collections. The painter William Morris Hunt was instrumental in assisting Boston collectors in the purchase of fine Impressionist works. These are now part of the collection and among the most popular pieces. The museum's Monets are surpassed only by those in Paris. Famed are the red- and black-figured vases and bronze and terra cotta statuettes from classical Greece and Rome; the collection of Egyptian Old Kingdom and Nubian art, second only to that of Cairo Museum; musical instruments; American fine and decorative arts; and the Asiatic art collection—the world's largest under a single roof. Artists and artisans—among them Paul Revere, John Singleton Copley, and John Singer Sargent—associated with Boston are well repre-

Isabella Stewart Gardner and Her Museum

Isabella Stewart Gardner was one interesting lady! Go to the Gardner Museum to see what she collected and built, but you will also see what is effectively a portrait of an eccentric with flair.

Popularly known as "Mrs. Jack" from her husband's first name, she was a New Yorker who married into an established, wealthy Boston family. That made her position in proper Boston society strained. Because she was unconcerned with people's opinions and behaved outrageously, Boston was outraged (and bemused). She walked a lion on a leash down Boston's fashionable streets. As an ostentatiously devout Episcopalian (after a bout of Buddhism), she regularly scoured the steps leading up to her church as penance. Her detractors said that, for her sins, she should have washed the whole church! Despite her romantic wanderings, her husband doted on her and she seemingly loved him. She was an enthusiast for art and beauty and collected selectively with the assistance of her protege, the famed Bernard Berenson.

She conceived of and had built her three-story 1901 Venetian palazzo home—now the museum—after her husband's death. It was a place to display her art collection and hold social events, but it was principally a place to showcase *her*. The Sargent portrait of her on display which was deemed scandalous in 1888, is beautiful and provides an arresting view of the lady. Her collection of 2,500 objects from three millennia is great. Many are masterpieces of the first order. The enclosed central garden atrium is breathtaking throughout the year. Most interesting is that she is still in charge. Nothing can be changed from the way she dictated that it be maintained. A still-unsolved 1990 robbery removed 13 works worth at least $200 million; their places remain empty except for explanatory notes.

sented as are objects associated with Boston's history and culture. Musical concerts and other cultural and social events are regularly held at the museum. Adjacent to the museum is the 1988 Tenshin-En Japanese Garden, a walled Japanese garden designed by Kyoto landscape architect Kinsaku Nakane, imitating New England's mountains, ocean, and islands.

➤Leave the museum and continue 0.2 mile along The Fenway to the Gardner Museum, which will be across the street to your left.

Veterans Memorial Park—a memorial to Boston's dead of World War II, Korea, and Vietnam—and Roberto Clemente Field, a baseball diamond named for the Puerto Rican ballplayer idolized by many, are nearby. Ahead along a greensward between divisions of Evans Way is the Massachusetts College of Art. Beyond it are Harvard Medical School, Children's Hospital, and Brigham & Woman's Hospital. Just right of Evans Way is the Isabella Stewart Gardner Museum.

➤Enter the Gardner Museum.

➤Leave the Gardner Museum, turn right, and go 0.15 mile on Louis Prang Street to Huntington (Avenue of the Arts).

➤Turn left on Huntington 0.2 mile to the Museum of Art T Stop, Green Line. Get on the T and return to the Hynes/ICA T Stop.

Walk 9

Jamaica Pond and Victorian Jamaica Plain/Jamaica Plain

General location: Boston's Jamaica Plain.

Special attractions: Quaint Victorian houses and a lovely walk along the banks and amid the greenery of Jamaica Pond.

Difficulty rating: Easy; flat terrain over good sidewalks.

Distance: 2 miles.

Estimated time: 1 hour.

Jamaica Pond and Victorian
Jamaica Plain/Jamaica Plain

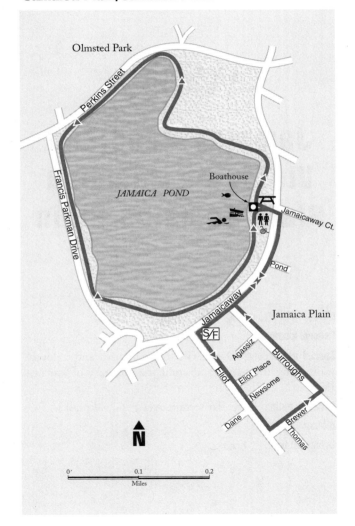

Services: Restrooms and water are available at the Jamaica Pond Boathouse. Food and drink are available in nearby Jamaica Plain Center.

Restrictions: None.

For more information: Contact Boston Parks and Recreation.

Getting started: Start at Eliot Street and Jamaicaway. Drivers access this walk from Boston and north via Boylston Street west, left onto Massachusetts Avenue, right onto Huntington Avenue, and left onto Jamaicaway to the start; from the south via U.S. Route 1 becoming Jamaicaway to the start; and from the west via MA Route 9 right onto Jamaicaway to the start. Park on the street.

Public transportation: Go to Forest Hills T Stop, Orange Line. Walk along South Street about half a mile to its continuation as Eliot Street. MBTA bus routes 38, 39, 41, and 48 stop at Eliot and Centre Streets 0.3 mile from the start.

Overview: This walk offers a view of some of Greater Boston's most interesting Victorian architecture as well as a leafy amble by a deep, clear pond.

Jamaica Plain is part of Roxbury. Roxbury is part of Boston. The area was settled in 1675, centered on an endowed school. The 1760 Loring-Greenough House, 12 South Street, and a 1769 Unitarian church, Center and Eliot Streets, are the oldest architectural survivors. In the mid-1800s, Jamaica Plain developed social cachet as a place where Boston society summered. At this time, its handsome Victorian houses were constructed while workers serving the gentry developed Jamaica Plain's "other side."

Jamaica Pond is a natural kettlehole or glacial pond. It is 54 feet deep and spring fed with a surface area of 65 acres. Its water is particularly clear and clean and was the source of Boston's water from 1795 to 1828 as well as for

Jamaica Pond and the Boathouse, Jamaica Plain.

ice—which was harvested each winter and stored for later use—in the 1870s. The pond is located in a park with a total area (both land and pond) of almost 110 acres. The pond has naturally occurring fish and other wildlife. It is stocked with trout twice a year.

Jamaica Pond and its park are part of Frederick Law Olmsted's Emerald Necklace. Purchased by Boston in 1890, the park was little changed from its natural condition by Olmsted, who made a walkway around the pond, removed existing structures, and built the 1912 Boathouse. The estate of Francis Parkman, Pinebanks, was preserved and survives in a state of ruin.

There is an outdoor theater—actually a dry glacial kettlehole—with summer theater. The Boathouse rents rowboats and sailboats. Picnicking and swimming from natural beaches are permitted and popular.

The Walk

➤Beginning at Jamaicaway's intersection with Eliot, walk down Eliot and stay left 0.2 mile to Brewer Street.

Along Eliot are some of Jamaica Plain's best Victorian buildings. At 1 Dane Street across Eliot is a Greek Revival house circa 1840 considered to be Jamaica Plain's finest Victorian. The 1832 Eliot School, 24 Eliot, is the 1689 school's successor with John Eliot's endowed gift to Roxbury. The building at 7 Eliot, circa 1855 (extensively remodeled in 1889), was the temporary town hall until 1868. Since 1878 it has been headquarters of the Footlight Club, American's oldest amateur theatrical group.

➤At Brewer, turn left 0.1 mile to and cross Burroughs Street.

Frederick Law Olmsted and the Emerald Necklace

Frederick Law Olmsted (1822–1903), known as America's first landscape architect, was the earliest, most influential, and active American designer of urban parks and green space as well as of gardens on private estates. Among his works is New York City's Central Park.

Nonetheless, Boston claims him. He designed Boston's Emerald Necklace, incorporating many pre-existing green spaces, some left virtually untouched. It consists of a connected nine-mile-long string of green parks and walking spaces of approximately 1,150 acres. Its segments, running from north to south, are Boston Common, the Public Garden, Commonwealth Avenue Mall, the Back Bay Fens, the Riverway, Olmsted Park, Jamaica Pond, Arnold Arboretum, and Franklin Park. It was not merely meant to assure the continued existence of urban parkland free of commercial development, but to deal with serious water control and health/pollution problems along its length that affected other areas of Boston. Many of Olmsted's Boston creations have been eliminated by time, new highways, effects of the Charles Dam, and other events. Many of the changes made to his work would have appalled him and are in defiance of his landscape design principles.

At his Brookline estate, Fairsted, 99 Warren Street, Olmsted lived from 1883 until his death in 1903. Fairsted is open to the public, is a ten-minute walk from Jamaica Pond, is beautifully landscaped, contains exhibits illustrating Olmsted's life and work, and is a National Historic Site. Olmsted and his successor firm, Olmsted Brothers, also created Dorchester Park, Doherty Park in Charlestown, and Wood Island Park (now gone) in East Boston. Arthur Shurcliff (1870–1957) trained under Olmsted and was responsible for modifying Olmsted-designed parks for twentieth-century needs.

Olmsted's Boston legacy endures in green space still enjoyed by thousands. His name is often invoked when new Boston green space is created.

Jamaica Plain's last surviving Gothic Revival house (circa 1850) is at 9 Brewer.

➤At Burroughs, turn left 0.2 mile to Jamaicaway.

Of interest are the 1896 Colonial Revival house and stable at No. 54 (owned by the Albanian Orthodox Diocese) and the impressive circa 1845 house at No. 50.

➤Turn right onto Jamaicaway 0.2 mile to Jamaicaway Court.

➤Turn left, cross Jamaicaway, and proceed 100 feet to Jamaica Pond Boathouse.

➤Turn right on the path along the pond's shoreline and follow it 1.25 miles.

➤Retrace your path 0.25 mile from the Boathouse to the start.

Walk 10

Arnold Arboretum/Jamaica Plain

General location: Jamaica Plain.

Special attractions: A vast botanical collection in a beautiful, spacious setting.

Difficulty rating: Easy but hilly with good concrete and gravel paths.

Distance: 4 miles.

Estimated time: 2 hours.

Arnold Arboretum/Jamaica Plain

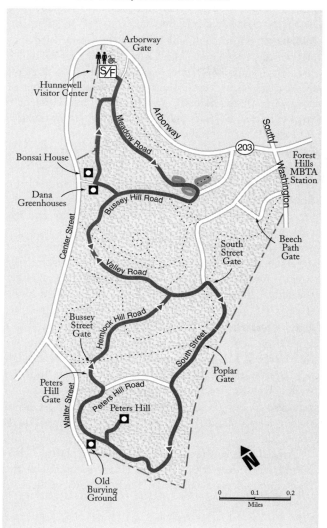

Services: Restrooms and water are available at the Hunnewell Visitor Center. Food and drink are available five blocks away at Jamaica Plain Center.

Restrictions: Motorized vehicles may enter only with special permits (available at the Visitor Center) for individuals with disabilities. Picnicking, fires, barbecues, dogs off leash, dog waste, bicycling off paved roads, removing or destroying plant material, and climbing trees (except a large cork tree, Boston's only public tree where climbing is authorized) are forbidden.

For more information: Contact Arnold Arboretum.

Getting started: Start at the Hunnewell Visitor Center. Drivers access this walk from Boston and north via Boylston Street west, left onto Massachusetts Avenue, right onto Huntington Avenue becoming Jamaicaway, and left onto Arborway; from the south via U.S. Route 1 and right onto Arborway; and from the west via MA Route 9 right onto Jamaicaway and right onto Arborway. Park on the street immediately upon turning on Arborway, enter through Arborway Gate, and follow Meadow Road to the start.

Public transportation: Orange Line T stops at the Forest Hills Stop, with access through the Beech Path Gate via South Street. MBTA bus routes 16, 21, 31, 32, 34 through 40, 42, 50, and 51 stop at Forest Hills T Stop. Join the walk on South Street and return to the same point.

Overview: Want a walk among greenery amid beautiful flowers and botanical specimens while learning? This is your walk!

Arnold Arboretum is a joint operation of Harvard University, with a lease through 2881 (Harvard maintains the landscape and plant collection), and the City of Boston,

Along a tree-lined path, Arnold Arboretum, Jamaica Plain.

whose Parks and Recreation Department is responsible for infrastructure.

The arboretum consists of 265 acres, including Peters Hill, Boston's highest elevation, and the Old Burying Ground, predating the park. More than 7,000 species of trees and shrubs are grouped by plant family for easy comparison, with groups arranged in botanical sequence along the main drive. Each plant is labeled by scientific and common name, country of origin, and collection accession number. The arboretum is a place for public enjoyment, an international center for research and education, and part of Olmsted's Emerald Necklace. It was begun in 1862 and named for its benefactor, James Arnold. The grounds were planned and designed by the arboretum's first director, Charles Sprague Sargent, and landscape architect Frederick Law Olmsted. A library and herbarium collections are maintained at the Visitors Center and in Harvard University's Cambridge Herbaria Building. Because plants change with the season, what is most interesting will differ from time to time. As a consequence, visitors are not limited by the suggested route. Walk a route appropriate for the day and season. Famous in season are the lilacs, rhododendrons, bonsai trees, Asiatic trees and shrubs along the Chinese Path, and rosaceous plants.

The Walk

➤At Hunnewell Visitor Center, view the exhibits and obtain information.

➤Exit the center to Meadow Road, turn right and continue 0.6 mile as it becomes Bussey Hill Road.

Dawn Redwoods are on your left. Arboretum agents found the tree, thought to be extinct, in China during

Of Interest

Boston's Cemeteries

Boston assumes municipal responsibility for 16 historical cemeteries and 3 active ones. Gravestone rubbing is forbidden. These cemeteries illustrate America's changing attitudes about graveyards and death. Seventeenth-century graveyards were merely places to dispose of the dead. Gravestones were *memento mori* to warn the living of their ultimate fate. The dead were happy in a better place. Their corpses were unimportant. Eighteenth-century gravestones reminded posterity that the dead had once existed. With time, they glorified the deceased and not always accurately. As dying moved from homes among families to hospitals among professionals, death became embarrassing. Cemeteries, such as Cambridge's Mount Auburn, were landscaped gardens and gravestones were tasteful decorative sculpture. Gravestones shrank in size and height so that they did not detract from enjoyment of the garden and to permit efficient maintenance of it. If not out of mind, the dead are now clearly intended to be out of sight.

World War II and propagated it at the arboretum. Near the end of Meadow Road is the famed collection of roses.

➤Continue 0.4 mile as the road climbs Bussey Hill.

Lilacs are on your left. Lilac Sunday at the arboretum, on the Sunday in May nearest the 15th, is a big deal. Much of Boston comes to see the 100 lilac varieties and 600 shrubs in bloom in varying shades of purple and white.

➤Turn right onto Valley Road and follow it 0.6 mile as it circles left to South Street.

Massive plantings of azaleas are on your left.

➤Turn right on South Street 0.3 mile to Poplar Gate.

➤Go through Poplar Gate 0.2 mile to Peters Hill Road. Rhododendrons are on the hillside to your right.

➤Turn left and walk 0.5 mile to a path leading to the hill's top. Take it to the end and return, a 0.1-mile loop.

Peters Hill, at 235 feet above sea level, is the highest point in Boston. Views from the top are worth seeing.

➤Turn right and continue 0.3 mile until you can turn left to Peters Hill Gate.

Immediately upon rejoining Peters Hill Road, Old Burying Ground is to your left.

➤Turn right and go through nearby Bussey Street Gate to Hemlock Hill Road.

➤Turn right and continue 0.4 mile to Valley Road. Rhododendrons are on your right at several points.

➤Turn left and continue 0.4 mile to Valley's juncture with Bussey Hill Road.

➤Turn left on Bussey Hill Road 0.2 mile to the path to the Dana Greenhouses and the Bonsai House.

➤Turn left 0.1 mile to and enter the greenhouses and the Bonsai House.

➤At the Bonsai House, join the path following the arboretum's northern perimeter past honeysuckles and cork trees to Meadow Road near the Visitor Center.

➤Return to the start.

Walk 11

Along the Charles River/Boston-Cambridge

General location: Charles River's banks near Back Bay and the MIT campus.

Special attractions: People watching, greenery and statuary, the Charles River, the Hatch Shell, the Museum of Science, Hayden Planetarium, the Mabar Omni Theatre, CambridgeGalleria, and the MIT campus.

Difficulty rating: Easy; flat terrain, good paths, and bridge ramp access.

Distance: 3.75 miles.

Along the Charles River/Boston-Cambridge

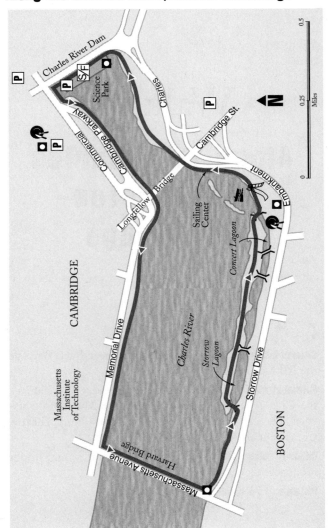

Estimated time: 1 hour 50 minutes.

Services: Restrooms and water are available at the CambridgeGalleria and the Science Museum. Food and drink are available throughout.

Restrictions: None.

For more information: Contact Boston Parks and Recreation.

Getting started: Start at Science Park. Drivers access this walk by I-90 to I-93/Central Artery exit 26 to Storrow Drive and follow the signs to Science Park/Charles River Dam with the start to your left on the dam. Covered commercial parking (wheelchair accessible, clearance 7 feet) is available by Science Park on your left. Pedestrian garage access is from the dam.

Public transportation: Go to Science Park T Stop, Green Line.

Overview: The Charles River is beautiful, historic, conveniently located, and great people-watching territory. Sunsets over the river from Boston are often beautiful. Early mornings are special, too. Sail or visit a museum or MIT campus along your route. Get away to a great place in the middle of a great city!

The Charles River, dividing Boston from Cambridge and still a vital Boston presence, and its adjacent bays and swamps defined Boston's earliest parameters and perimeters. Its 80-mile length is much changed from its original condition. It has been dammed, its banks shored and changed, and much of its breadth filled in and built on. The Charles River Basin, the river's most popular and heavily trafficked part, is a 9-mile length stretching from the Watertown Dam to the Charles Dam. It was created in 1910 with construction of the lower dam—where the Museum of Science is—to prevent tidal flow from Boston

Harbor going up the river to undermine riverbanks and threaten Back Bay, which was always perilously close to inundation—particularly during storms. Locks on the dam permitted boats to enter and leave the basin from and to Boston Harbor. Since 1981, a new dam about a half mile farther down the river has eliminated Charles Dam's tidal containment function. There is constant activity—birdlife, sculling, sailing, sailboarding, rowing, the annual Head of the Charles Regatta, etc.—on the water; biking, jogging, walking, in-line skating, and much more—sometimes very much more—along its banks; and even underwater, when herring make their spawning run up and over the Watertown Dam in May.

The Walk

➤Exit Science Park T Stop, turn toward the Cambridge riverbank, and stay left on the Charles Dam.

The stone architectural features piled along the Boston shoreline are remnants of demolished West End buildings.

➤See the Museum of Science/Hayden Planetarium/Mabar Omni Theatre. They comprise a popular Boston tourist site.

➤Cross the dam 0.1 mile to the Cambridge side.

Look to the Cambridge shore for crew boathouses and the statue of Athena atop an old children's publishing house.

➤Turn left and stay left on the Cambridge Parkway/Memorial Drive bike/pedestrian path along the river 1.3 miles to Massachusetts Avenue.

Looking across the Charles River to Boston's Back Bay, Cambridge.

Across Commercial Avenue on your right is CambridgeGalleria. Farther along on your right is the Massachusetts Institute of Technology campus (for MIT campus, see Walk 12).

➤Turn left on Harvard Bridge and stay left 0.3 mile over the river (see Walk 12).

From the bridge much can be seen, including baseball's Fenway Park—you can see its lights by the Citgo sign—Bunker Hill Monument, and the State House dome. The plaque near the end on the left is in honor of Harry Houdini, the escape artist, who performed one of his feats near this point.

➤Turn left near the end of the bridge and move down the ramp leading to the water's edge.

➤Follow the path with the river immediately on your left 1.9 miles. This runs along the Esplanade. It is crowded with joggers, bicyclers, walkers, skatebladers, and everyone else, but there is ample room. Spot double-crested cormorants on the water. View fabulous sunsets across it.

The embankment adjacent to the Beacon Hill Flats and continuing to the islands and lagoons and surrounding mainland between the Charles River and Storrow Drive in Back Bay is called the Esplanade. It is a very popular place. Much of interest happens there, including performances at the Hatch Shell and sailing, kayaking, and sailboarding from the sailing center on its shore.

When established, the Esplanade's purpose—as the name implies—was for social arm-in-arm promenades and evening constitutionals. The riverbank was extended along what is now the Esplanade, with a promenade of 100 feet, in 1893. The Storrow Embankment created a broad strip of land that permitted the creation of a riverine parkland (completed in 1931), based loosely upon that of the Alster Basin of Hamburg, Germany. The building of Storrow Drive in 1951 did much to diminish, but not to destroy, the beauty of the Esplanade.

On the river are birdlife, rowing shells, and sailboats. Along the way will be many monuments and statues of interest, including a huge stylized head of Arthur "Pops" Fiedler, for five decades the imperious head of the Boston Pops. The 1929 Edward Hatch Memorial Shell is the scene of many performances and of the Fourth of July free open-air concert with fabulous fireworks attended by up to half a million people. Near the sailing school (open to the public) is the island where *Make Way for Ducklings'* Mrs. Mallard hatched her young. The Esplanade Cafe— really a snack shop—and a children's playground are near here. You will pass under the Longfellow Bridge, known as "the salt and pepper shakers" for reasons that will be obvious when you see it. A swimming pool lies beyond it.

➤Enter the ramp to your left leading to the dam.

Note the locks that permit boats to pass through.

➤Continue 0.1 mile to the start.

Walk 12

Massachusetts Avenue/Boston-Cambridge

General location: Massachusetts Avenue from Symphony Hall, Boston, to Harvard Square, Cambridge.

Special attractions: Symphony Hall, Horticultural Hall, the First Church of Christ Scientist, Harvard Bridge and the Charles River, the MIT campus and museum, Central Square, Harvard Square, and the urban sights and sounds along the way.

Difficulty rating: Easy; flat terrain over good sidewalks but lengthy and heavily trafficked.

Massachusetts Avenue/Boston-Cambridge

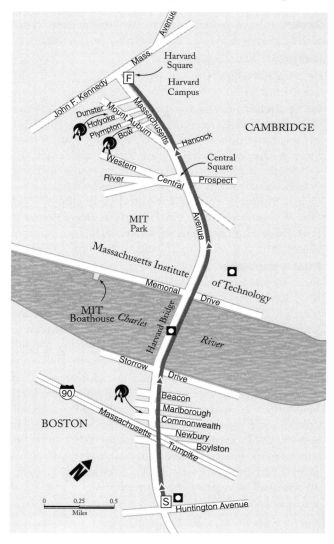

Distance: 3 miles.

Estimated time: 1.5 hours.

Services: Restrooms and water are available at commercial establishments. Food and drink are available throughout.

Restrictions: None.

For more information: Contact the First Church of Christ Scientist or MIT.

Getting started: Start across Massachusetts Avenue from Symphony Hall. Drivers access this walk from I-90 by exit 21, otherwise from I-93/Central Artery by exit 26 onto Storrow Drive and then left, onto Massachusetts Avenue, and south to Huntington Avenue. Commercial parking (wheelchair accessible, clearance 6 feet) is available at Prudential Center by turning left onto Huntington to Prudential Center on your left. Pedestrian garage access is from either Huntington or Boylston Street. Turn right on Huntington and walk three blocks to the start.

Public transportation: Arrive at Symphony/Auditorium T Stop, Green Line, and return from Harvard Square T Stop, Red Line. MBTA bus route 1 continually travels the length of Massachusetts between the start and end of the walk, making many stops en route, and should be used to return directly to the start or otherwise modify the full walk. MBTA route 39 also stops at Symphony Hall.

Overview: This walk takes you along one of Boston's major thoroughfares, Massachusetts Avenue, from Symphony Hall/Christian Science Mother Church to Harvard University, while crossing the Charles River and taking you past the MIT campus, much interesting architecture, the sites of many interesting and historical events, and varied peoples and neighborhoods. This is an excellent "rubbing-elbows" walk along busy streets offering a smorgasbord of sights and sounds.

The Walk

►Start across Massachusetts Avenue from Symphony Hall, a 1900 building by McKim, Mead and White and home of the Boston Symphony Orchestra.

Horticultural Hall of 1901 immediately to your rear is a grandiose English Baroque building and home of the Horticultural Society, founded in 1829 to advance the knowledge and practice of horticulture. The society holds an annual spring flower show and has an extensive horticultural library.

►Turn right, stay right, and go .09 mile to Harvard Bridge.

Christian Science World Headquarters is on your right. The original, modest 1893 Romanesque stone church is now a chapel behind the huge 1905 basilica that houses the largest organ in the Western Hemisphere and seats 5,000. I. M. Pei and Partners added to the complex's monumentality around 1970 with the World Headquarters building and a Massachusetts Avenue limestone plaza entrance that includes a 700-foot reflecting pool, once part of the air conditioning system but now an architectural ornament. The tower beside the reflecting pool and the low-lying building on the other side are identical geometrical figures, one erect, the other prone. The complex houses offices for the sect's worldwide functions, the daily *Christian Science Monitor* newspaper, and the administration of the Mother Church. Regular tours, including the Bible collection and Maparium, are given.

Christian Science developed locally. Mary Baker Eddy—the Longyear Museum and Historical Society maintains several Boston-area buildings associated with her—created it and, through her 1866 book, *Christian Science and Health with Key to the Scriptures,* described its fundamentals—no-

The Mother Church of First Church of Christ, Scientist, Boston.

tably that prayer and a proper understanding of Christian principles provide health and curing and obviate the need for conventional medical assistance, whose use is contrary to scriptural authority.

The Performance Center of Berklee College of Music—called the "Juilliard of Jazz"—is at 236 Massachusetts.

Tower Records—popular with younger or musically inclined walkers—is at 360 Newbury Street in a 1918 building radically renovated to its present stylish form in 1989 by Frank O. Gehry.

The 1882 Ames Mansion at 355 Commonwealth is modeled on French Loire Valley chateaux. One of the largest Back Bay homes, it had opulent interiors.

Across Massachusetts is Eliot Hotel, recently renovated and the site of Clio, among the trendiest of Boston restaurants.

To the right at 483 Beacon Street, the Hotel Cambridge—distinguishable by its "H-C" monogram on each side of the pediment—was a large 1898 Willard T. Sears apartment hotel.

Across Beacon is Church Court, the site of the 1891 Mount Vernon Church that was destroyed in a 1978 fire, which incorporates portions of the church's surviving ruins.

➤Cross Harvard Bridge 0.5 mile on the right (see Walk 11).

Harvard Bridge is 364.4 smoots and one ear long—a figure annually repainted on the bridge. In 1958, the eponymous Oliver R. Smoot, an MIT fraternity pledge, was rolled the length of the bridge—whether voluntarily is not recorded—and the measurement thereby determined. The "ear" reflects that his ear was partially severed in the process and was added to the measurement as compensation.

Boston's Architects

There are three Boston architectural schools: MIT, Harvard, and Boston Architectural Center. MIT's, dating from 1868, was America's first.

Buildings by Peter Harrison—America's first professional architect—still stand. Alexander Parris developed the "Boston granite style" for commercial buildings. Samuel McIntire's surviving Salem houses speak eloquently of his skills. Asher Benjamin was nationally influential through his books of architectural designs. Solomon Willard designed some of Boston's best-known landmarks, including Bunker Hill Monument. Self-taught Ralph Adams Cram was responsible for making "Gothic" America's standard for university campuses and monumental churches.

Described elsewhere are the architects Charles Bulfinch, whose early-eighteenth-century buildings were inspired; Henry Hobson Richardson, a master of the latter eighteenth century; and the New York architectural firm of McKim, Mead and White. Each did much to give Boston its present appearance. Also described elsewhere, but often mistakenly overlooked in any discussion of Boston's architects, are interior designers, particularly Ogden Codman, Jr., John LaFarge, and Louis Comfort Tiffany, and landscape designers, particularly Frederick Law Olmsted.

Walter Gropius, founder in 1919 of the Bauhaus school, fled the Nazis and came to Harvard with some of his students, including Mies van der Rohe. Jose Luis Sert came to teach at MIT and started his own architectural firm. I. M. Pei was schooled at MIT and served on the faculty at Harvard.

Famous modern architects' works around Boston include the only American work of LeCorbusier, who taught at Harvard, and several Eero Saarinen designs.

Louis Sullivan—creator of the steel-frame skyscraper—was Boston bred but not a Boston architect. He left MIT and Boston in a trail of disparaging comments. Buckminster Fuller was born in Milton and expelled—twice—from Harvard. Frank Lloyd Wright lived in Weymouth as a child during his father's peripatetic travels as a Methodist minister.

➤Stay right on Massachusetts 1.6 miles to Harvard Square.

On your right and left is the campus of the Massachusetts Institute of Technology (MIT). Its Hart Nautical Museum has many ship models and appeals to sailing buffs.

MIT possesses an excellent variety of great buildings. MIT campus's signature structures are the 1915 MacLaurin and Rogers buildings. Their two Pantheon-inspired domes and the Ionic portico are famous and closely identified with MIT. Their interiors are less successful. Eero Saarinen designed the 1955 Kresge Auditorium and Kresge Chapel. Each is distinctive and sinuous inside and out, and the two work well together. Alvar Aalto was responsible for the 1948 Baker House. It is interesting for its rippling facade but fits poorly with uncomfortably near neighbors. I. M. Pei and Partners created the 1963 Green Building, the 1969 Dreyfus Building, the 1975 Landau Chemical Engineering Building, and the 1985 Wiesner Building. All are interesting. Each is different.

Also on campus are major works of art, such as Henry Moore's 1976 *Three-Piece Reclining* and 1963 *Reclining Figure,* Alexander Calder's 1965 *The Big Sail,* Louise Nevelson's 1975 *Transparent Horizon,* and Pablo Picasso's 1963 *Figure découpée.*

On your left at No. 254 is the NECCO factory—where they make those little multicolored candy discs—and on your right is the MIT Museum at No. 265—a small but great place, if grim in external appearance, for the technically-oriented. At No. 740 is the site of Elias Howe's workshop, where he invented the sewing machine in 1844–1855.

As you continue, you are entering prime people-watching and ethnic-restaurant territory. On the crowded street are faces and voices from all over the world.

You will pass through Central Square. Go past the 1890 Cambridge City Hall at No. 795, the 1881 terra cotta-and-brick First Baptist Church, Cambridge—the congregation has been here since 1817 and its front rose window is noteworthy—at 5 Magazine, and the 1868 neo-Gothic Old Cambridge Baptist Church at No. 1151—its large stained glass window facing the street is an early Tiffany in a unique style. Enter the penumbra of Harvard University.

As you near Harvard Square, you will notice the change from earthy immigrant to often equally earthy undergraduate. Bookstores, old and used, proliferate. A place for a moderately priced, tasty, and highly amusing meal is Mr. and Mrs. Bartley's Burger Cottage. Upstairs at the Hasty Pudding, a restaurant atop the home of the student theatrical group that gives famous, ironic, annual acting awards, is at No. 10 Holyoke just off Massachusetts.

►This walk ends at Harvard Square. Take MBTA bus route 1 directly back to the start or go to the nearby T stop.

Walk 13

Cambridge

General location: Cambridge, immediately north of Boston, around Harvard University.

Special attractions: Harvard University and historical Cambridge.

Difficulty rating: Easy but lengthy; flat terrain and good sidewalks.

Distance: 4 miles.

Estimated time: 2 hours.

Services: Restrooms and water are available at museums and commercial establishments. Food and drink are available throughout.

Restrictions: None.

For more information: Contact the Harvard Square Information Booth or Harvard University.

Cambridge

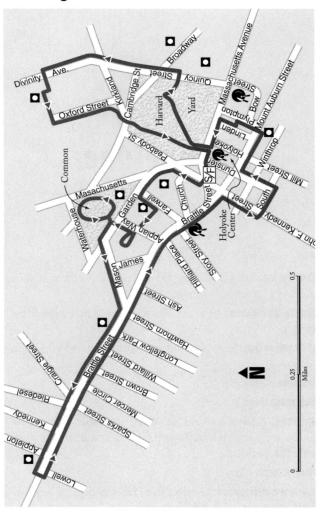

Getting started: Start at Harvard Square T Stop, Red Line. Drivers access this walk from Boston and south via I-90 exit 21, or I-93/Central Artery exit 26 to Storrow Drive, onto Massachusetts Avenue north over Harvard Bridge to Harvard Square, Cambridge. From the west go via MA Route 2 to and then left on John F. Kennedy Street to Harvard Square. From the north go via U.S. Route 3 continuing on MA Route 2A (Massachusetts Avenue) to Harvard Square. Commercial covered parking is available (wheelchair accessible, clearance 6 feet 2 inches) by continuing east on Massachusetts for a block past Harvard Square T Stop to and right a block on Dunster Street, left a block on Mount Auburn Street, and left on Holyoke Street half a block to Holyoke Center immediately on the left. Pedestrian garage access is from Holyoke. To get to the start, turn left on Holyoke to nearby Massachusetts, then left two blocks on Massachusetts.

Public transportation: Go to Harvard Square T Stop, Red Line. MBTA bus routes 1, 64, 66, 68, 69, 71 through 75, 77, 78, 86, and 96 stop at Harvard Square.

Overview: This walk is fascinating for those interested in Harvard, museums of many sorts, architecture, and colonial/Revolutionary history.

"Newtowne" was established by Massachusetts Bay Colony's founders in 1630 across the Charles River from Boston as the colony's first seat of government. Harvard College was formed there in 1636, but was not known by that name until 1638. When the college was renamed, the many Puritan Cambridge University graduates successfully insisted that the village's name be changed to Cambridge. The early settlement's form survives largely intact in Harvard Square. In 1775, militias from throughout New England gathered on Cambridge Common. In July of that year, George Washington took command of the Continental Army. General Washington kept his headquarters in Cambridge—in Harvard buildings, made available to the American army while the college moved to Watertown—until the British evacuated Boston in March 1776. With construction after the Revolution of bridges spanning the Charles River, Cambridge became accessible to Boston and vice versa. Immigrants arrived, empty parts were occupied and developed, and Cambridge was incorporated as a city in 1846. Cambridge has long been home to a significant African-American community. Modern Cambridge, with a resident student population of about 100,000, is largely defined by its institutions of higher learning, Harvard and MIT. Nonetheless, it has historically been a manufacturing and commercial center. It is now a high-technology industrial area.

The Walk

➤From Harvard Square T Stop, go to the Out of Town News kiosk on the same traffic island.

Nearby is Dimitri Hadzi's 1985 *Omphalos* statue, a 21-foot-tall granite structure whose name is a reference to Delphi in ancient Greece, the navel of the Earth and entrance to divine knowledge. Harvard has no statue dedicated to Humility.

➤Cross Brattle Street and John F. Kennedy/Peabody Streets, turn right, stay left on Peabody, stop in front of Harvard Coop, then continue 0.1 mile to Massachusetts Avenue.

Across Peabody the first popularly elected constitutional convention met in 1779 in the Fourth Meetinghouse and wrote the world's oldest constitution. It was the model for the U.S. Constitution and is still in effect as Massachusetts's constitution.

To your left on Church Street is the wooden 1833 Gothic Revival First Parish Church.

➤Continue to and go left on Garden Street 0.1 mile to Farwell Place.

Known as "God's Acre," Old Burying Grounds on your left was established in 1635. Among those buried here are America's first printer, Stephen Daye; early Harvard presidents; and soldiers of the Revolution—including the black Patriots Cato Stedman and Neptune Frost.

Slightly farther on your left is Christ Church. Designed by Peter Harrison, it is Cambridge's oldest (1761) surviving church. When its Tory congregation fled in 1774, Connecticut troops used it as a barracks and its organ pipes were melted to make bullets. It reopened for services on New Year's Eve, 1775, when George and Martha Washington were among the worshipers.

➤Follow the path between Christ Church and Old Burying Grounds to Farwell and follow it about a half block. Stop at the house on your right.

This is the 1827 Nichols House of John Nichols, a Civil War Union Army surgeon.

➤Follow the brick path to the right of Nichols House to a small courtyard.

On your right is circa 1772 Read House, one of the few surviving Cambridge houses of a Patriot soldier. James Read was a tanner and was with the Cambridge militia on the day of the battles of Lexington-Concord.

➤Continue along the brick path to and cross Appian Way.

➤Turn right and stay left a short distance to Radcliffe Yard, visible through the gate in the brick wall on your left. Enter.

In Radcliffe Yard, Fay House (1807), originally a Federal-style private mansion, was the first Radcliffe College building. Nearby are three linked buildings—Hemenway Gymnasium of 1898, the 1904 Agassiz House, and the 1909 Schlesinger Library on the History of Women, including a vast collection of culinary literature. These three structures are, collectively, important examples of Colonial Revival architecture.

➤Return to Appian Way, turn left, stay left to and cross Garden 0.1 mile, and enter Cambridge Common.

First set aside for grazing cattle, training militia, and holding public meetings in 1631, it was originally four times its present size of 16 acres. For over 350 years, it has been Cambridge's focal point for religious, social, and political activity. Once crossed by thoroughfares, the Common was enclosed as a public park in 1830.

It was the encampment and training ground for Washington's Continental Army. By some accounts, Washington assumed command of the Continental Army under the Washington Elm—it fell in 1923 and that now growing is its offspring—on the Common on July 3, 1775. On a traffic island near the Common are cast hoofprints representing the path of William Dawes, Paul Revere's unsung fellow rider. Three British cannons captured in 1775 are to the left of the 1869 Civil War monument.

At 9 Waterhouse Street stands the 1753 Waterhouse House, home of Dr. Benjamin Waterhouse who introduced smallpox vaccine to America in 1800. Near the same corner of the Common and across Massachusetts is Harvard Law School.

➤Exit the Common as you entered it and stay right on and cross Garden 0.1 mile at its intersection with Mason Street.

Before you to your right is First Church Congregational (1872). Along with the Parish Unitarian Universalist, it is the oldest congregation in Cambridge. (The two congregations were one until the early nineteenth century, when they divided over a religious controversy.) The 1721 gilded weathercock atop the tower was made by famed weathervane crafter Shem Drowne.

➤Stay right on Mason 0.2 mile to Brattle, nicknamed "Tory Row" prior to the Revolution for the wealthy British loyalists dwelling along it.

➤Turn right and stay right on Brattle a short distance.

On your right is Hastings House (1845), housing the Harvard Divinity School faculty.

Near 76 Brattle (follow a brick wall on the right down a small footpath to the rear), is a pair of plaques in English and Braille that were dedicated by the deaf and blind Helen Keller to honor her teacher, Anne Sullivan, at Sullivan's childhood home.

➤Continue about two blocks to Longfellow House, 105 Brattle.

This is an elaborate, elegant 1759 Georgian mansion attributed to architect Peter Harrison and built as the mansion of John Vassall, Jr., a loyalist and wealthy West Indian plantation owner. When Vassall fled with the Revolution, Washington made it his personal quarters during the siege of Boston. Henry Wadsworth Longfellow first rented rooms here in 1837 and bought it for his home when he married in 1843. Longfellow's descendants gave it to the U.S. National Park Service in 1974.

➤ Stay right about half a mile past Appleton Street to the 1688 Hooper-Lee-Nichols House, 159 Brattle, on your right.

Another Loyalist mansion, this—now the offices of the Cambridge Historical Society—is one of the two oldest surviving homes in Cambridge. John Bartlett, author of *Bartlett's Familiar Quotations,* lived at No. 165.

➤ Cross Brattle, turn left, stay right, and retrace your path a half mile to the corner of Hawthorn Street, across from Hastings House.

On your right is the Henry Vassall House. At least the chimney dates from the mid-seventeenth century, but the house was thoroughly remodeled in the eighteenth century. When the Vassalls fled with the Revolution's outbreak, it was used as the Continental Army's medical headquarters.

➤ Stay right 0.1 mile to the intersection with Ash Street.

At 90 Brattle is H. H. Richardson's 1883 Stoughton House. T. S. Eliot lived at 16 Ash.

➤ Continue 0.2 mile, passing on your right Loeb Drama Center (1959)—noted for its innovative flexible stage and as the location of the American Repertory Theatre—to the 1808 Dexter Pratt Home, 56 Brattle, at the intersection with Story Street.

Set back from the street behind a terrace, it now houses, among other things, the Blacksmith House Pastry and Cafe. Dexter Pratt was the village blacksmith immortalized by Longfellow's poem. A granite marker indicates the site of the poem's "spreading chestnut tree." Dimitri Gerakaris's 1989 forged steel and bronze sculpture affixed to the house's wall memorializes it. A chair made from the tree is at Longfellow House.

Massachusetts Hall, Harvard University, Cambridge.

➤Continue a short distance to across from the corner of Church and Brattle.

On your right is Brattle House (1727), another Tory home abandoned by its owner with the Revolution and used by the Continental Army for quartering its commissary general.

➤Continue and stay with Brattle's continuation as Mount Auburn Street 0.1 mile when Brattle turns sharply left.

On your right is Winthrop Square, now a park but in the seventeenth and eighteenth centuries the town market.

➤Turn right down John F. Kennedy and stay right 0.1 mile to and cross South Street.

On your right is the 1762 Hicks House owned by the carpenter John Hicks, reputedly a Boston Tea Party participant and a Patriot soldier killed by British soldiers retreating from the battles of Lexington-Concord.

➤Turn left onto South and stay right a block to and cross Dunster.

➤Turn left and stay right two blocks to Mount Auburn.

➤Turn right and stay right three blocks to Plympton Street.

On your left is the 1909 Castle, home of *The Lampoon,* a Harvard student humor magazine. The building is as zany as the magazine. It is a cylindrical tower, and on its front one can readily see eyes (two round windows), a nose (the center window), a mouth (the door), and a hat (the domed roof). An ibis, the magazine's mascot, is on the roof.

➤Turn left, stay left, and go about half a block to a gate on your left by a granite marker for Apthorp House.

➤Enter the gate and follow the path to the front of a white wood frame house.

This is the 1760 Apthorp House. Built for the first rector of Christ Church, East Apthorp, it was thought by Puritans to be so lavish it was referred to as the Bishop's Palace. The controversy was so intense that Apthorp returned to England. During the Siege of Boston, Continental Army troops were quartered in the house, and the British General Burgoyne and his officers stayed there after their defeat by Americans at Saratoga.

➤Cross the courtyard and turn right after the Linden Street gate.

➤Stay right on Linden half a block to Massachusetts, turn left, and stay left a little more than a block.

At 10 Holyoke to your left is the 1889 Hasty Pudding Clubhouse with a restaurant on its top floor. The club is the oldest continuous U.S. theatrical organization and the world's third oldest. It is famous for its annual ironic awards (and accompanying parades) given to famous actors and actresses. To your left is the entrance to Holyoke Center Plaza and Harvard Information Center. Across Massachusetts is Wadsworth House (1726), a yellow frame house built by the colonial legislature as the official residence for Harvard presidents and occupied by nine of them and—briefly—by George Washington.

➤Cross to Wadsworth House and enter Harvard Yard through a gate between Wadsworth House and Lehman Hall.

In front of University Hall is Daniel Chester French's 1884 statue of John Harvard—known popularly as the "three lies" because its inscription says "John Harvard, Founder, 1638." John Harvard did not found Harvard, which was founded in 1636. The likeness is not that of

Harvard University

Harvard College, not its original name, was founded in Cambridge in 1636—it's the oldest U.S. college. It was renamed in honor of John Harvard, a young cleric and graduate of Cambridge University, because upon his death in Charlestown in 1638, he left to it half his fortune and his library of 302 books. His library burned, along with Harvard Hall, in 1764 save one book improperly removed the night of the fire by a student. When the student returned it, the college president thanked him for saving it and expelled him for having taken it.

Harvard's heart is Harvard Yard, parts of which date from the 1630s. All freshmen are housed in it. In Harvard Yard are many of Harvard's oldest and most important buildings. Bulfinch's granite University Hall (1813–1815) divides the "old" from the "new" Harvard Yards. Annual Harvard commencements are held each June in the "new" yard before University Hall. The original college building was in the middle of a cow "yard" or pasture. Harvard Yard's surrounding brick wall is perforated by nine major and several smaller gates. Access is generally unrestricted.

There are about 18,000 matriculating Harvard students at any one time. Famous Harvard graduates and faculty members—and even drop-outs such as Bill Gates—are numerous. Harvard College and Radcliffe College were long associated educational institutions. All Harvard students were men, all Radcliffe students women. Radcliffe, opened in 1879 as the Collegiate Institute for Women, was effectively Harvard's women's college. Harvard faculty taught Radcliffe students in separate classes until 1943. Thereafter, Radcliffe students were admitted and taught as Harvard students but received degrees from Radcliffe.

Since 1998, both men and women are Harvard students and graduates.

Harvard's museums should not be missed, and a visit to its historical, beautiful campus is a delight.

John Harvard—whose appearance is a mystery except that he died of consumption, so the statue's legs are the thin, weakened ones of a tuberculosis sufferer—but of Sherman Hoar, a popular Class of 1882 member and friend of the artist. Rubbing Mr. Harvard's foot is thought to bring good luck.

You will pass through the "new" yard and return through the "old." In the new yard is Memorial Church (1931). Widener Library, named for Harry Elkins Widener, who died when the *Titanic* sank, is the third largest U.S. library and the world's largest university library; it is famed for its more than 4.5—by some counts 13—million books on more than 5 miles of shelves. Its principal designer was Julian Francis Abele, the first African-American graduate of Paris's Ecole des Beaux Arts and chief designer of a number of memorable buildings of the period. Inside along the main staircase are the murals *Death and Victory* and *The Coming of Americans to Europe* by John Singer Sargent, described by one critic as "probably the very worst works of public art ever done by a major American painter." Widener is but one of 90 libraries at Harvard. Two immediately adjacent to it are the Pusey Library, containing among other things a noted collection of theatrical costumes and memorabilia, and the Houghton Library, which is the principal Harvard rare book, manuscript, and portrait painting repository. Sever Hall (1878) is a jarringly out-of-place but excellent Romanesque work by Richardson.

➤Complete an easterly transit of the yard, pass through the nearby gate, cross, and turn left on Quincy Street.

William, Henry, and Alice James shared a house, now the Harvard Faculty Club, at 20 Quincy. Immediately around you are the Carpenter Center for the Visual Arts (1961), the only North American building designed by the Swiss architect LeCorbusier, who also taught at Harvard; the Fogg Art Museum; the Busch-Reisinger Museum in Otto Werner Hall—generally of Germanic art; and the Sackler Museum—mostly Asian art and performing the public exhibition function of the Fogg Art Museum. Visit them.

➤Go to and cross Cambridge Street 0.2 mile to the 1969 Graduate School of Design's Gund Hall.

➤Turn left on Cambridge a short distance to Memorial Hall (1874).

This is William Ware/Henry Van Brunt's massive brick memorial to Harvard's 136 Union Civil War dead—the 64 dead Confederate graduates are unmemorialized, if not unmourned—in a Ruskin Gothic style. It now serves as a dining hall, student commons, and performing theater. Its appearance is that of a Gothic cathedral. It has Tiffany and La Farge stained glass windows.

➤Return along Cambridge to and cross Quincy again.

➤Turn left on Quincy and stay right 0.1 mile to Kirkland Street.

➤Cross to Divinity Avenue, Quincy's continuation, and stay right 0.2 mile to the 1889 Semitic Museum and its adjacent Natural and Cultural History Museums, including the fabulous Ware Collection of glass botanical specimens, on your left.

➤From any of these museums, go to and cross Oxford Street, immediately paralleling Quincy on the west, turn left, stay right, and pass between Memorial Hall and the Harvard Science Center along Kirkland for 0.3 mile.

The center was designed by José Luis Sert, a Spaniard who headed Harvard's Graduate School of Design and whose own interesting house is nearby behind a brick wall at 64 Francis Street. The center's hi-tech but naturalistic Tanner Fountain, which languidly expels sometimes mist and sometimes steam, is fascinating.

➤Cross Cambridge, re-enter Harvard Yard, and pass through the "old" yard. Massachusetts Hall (1718) is Harvard's oldest surviving building and was a Patriot barracks during the Siege of Boston. "A" Harvard Hall housed Harvard's first classroom but this 1764 building is the third of that name. Hollis Hall (1762) was the dormitory quarters of Charles Bulfinch, Ralph Waldo Emerson, and Henry David Thoreau. The dents on the steps and bricks in front are the results of cannonballs thrown by students from dormitory windows. During winter, students heated cannonballs in their fireplaces—then the only sources of heat. Hot cannonballs emitted warmth during the night. With spring, students tossed the unneeded cannonballs from their windows to the pavement below. Also among these older buildings are the small Georgian Holden Chapel (1742) and Bulfinch's Stoughton Hall (1804).

➤Leave Harvard Yard, retracing your route through the gate near Wadsworth House, cross and turn right on Massachusetts becoming Brattle, and stay left 0.1 mile to Peabody.

➤Turn left and return to the start.

Walk 14A

Boston Marathon:
Heartbreak Hill/Newton

General location: Immediately west of Boston, from Newton Lower Falls through Newton Centre.

Special attractions: Part of the Boston Marathon route—with Heartbreak Hill and the *Young at Heart* statue, plus Newton's pleasant streets and Boston College campus.

Difficulty rating: Moderate; lengthy, with hills and sidewalks sometimes becoming narrow gravel paths.

Distance: 5 miles.

Estimated time: 2.5 hours.

Services: Restrooms and water are available at the Newton Free Public Library. Food and drink are available beyond the walk's end.

Heartbreak Hill/Newton

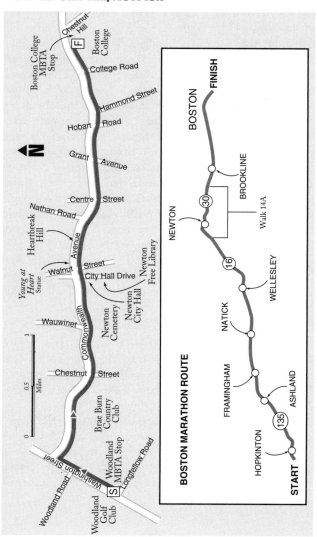

Restrictions: None.

For more information: Contact Boston Athletic Association or the Jimmy Fund Walk.

Getting started: Start at Woodland T Stop, Green Line. Drivers access this walk most interestingly by (a) from the west, beginning at the marathon's start in Hopkinton, Grover and East Main Streets, following MA Route 135—becoming West Union/Union Streets in Ashland—through Ashland, Framingham (Waverly Street), and Natick (West Central/Central Streets) to Wellesley where you leave Route 135 for MA Route 16 (Washington Street) and from there to the starting point in Newton Lower Falls or (b) from the east by generally reversing the marathon route from the finish line at Boston's Back Bay's Copley Square by going west on Boylston Street, turning right onto Massachusetts Avenue and left onto Beacon Street to Cleveland Circle, exiting onto Chestnut Hill Avenue and left onto MA Route 30 (Commonwealth Avenue), then left on MA Route 16 (Washington Street) to the starting point near Longfellow Road. Park on the street.

Public transportation: Start at Woodland T Stop and end at Boston College T Stop, Green Line.

Overview: This walk permits Boston Marathon enthusiasts to follow the most fabled part of its route—Heartbreak Hill—while enjoying a pleasant residential area and the Boston College campus.

The Boston Athletic Association (founded 1887) administers, and the Jimmy Fund organizes, annual walks of the route of the Boston Marathon. It is the world's oldest annual marathon (April 19, 1897); the only one always run on a Monday—it is held on Patriot's Day, formerly

April 19 but since 1969 that Massachusetts holiday is always April's third Monday; attracted the largest marathon field—38,708 in 1996; since 1990 is the only non-Olympic marathon prequalifying runners; and draws over 1,000,000 spectators annually. More than 100,000 runners have participated. Its route mirrors the terrain from Marathon to Athens in Greece. Beginning in Hopkinton, Grover and East Main Streets, it follows MA Route 135—becoming West Union/Union Streets in Ashland—through Ashland—Ashland's Metcalf's Mill was the starting line 1897–1923 until the course was lengthened, Framingham (Waverly), and Natick (West Central/Central Streets) to Wellesley. Here it leaves Route 135 for MA Route 16 (Washington). At Newton Lower Falls, it follows MA Route 30 (Commonwealth) past Boston College and enters Chestnut Hill. In Brookline at Cleveland Circle, it follows Beacon. At Boston's Kenmore Square, the route rejoins Commonwealth (inbound), turns right onto Hereford Street—against the normal flow of traffic—and then left onto Boylston to the finish line between Exeter and Dartmouth Streets by Boston Public Library.

The Walk

➤Exit Woodland T Stop, Newton Lower Falls near Wellesley, turn right and stay right 0.75 mile on Washington to Commonwealth.

Woodland Golf Club is on your left.

➤Turn right on Commonwealth and stay right 1.9 miles to Walnut Street.

Pass Brae Burn Country Club and Newton Cemetery on your right. On the right at City Hall Drive is Newton

The Young at Heart *statue, Boston Marathon route, Newton.*

City Hall and War Memorial and adjacent to it is the Newton Free Public Library.

➤At Walnut on the left is Rich Munro's 1993 bronze *Young at Heart* statue of the youthful Johnny "the Elder" Kelley shaking hands with his aged self, both marathon runners.

Johnny Adelbert Kelley's association with the Boston Marathon is legendary. He is referred to as "the Elder" because another, younger, unrelated Johnny Kelley is also famed in Boston Marathon annals. It is Johnny "the Elder" Kelley's statue—actually his double statue—in front of you.

He ran—and completed—his last full marathon in 1992 at the age of 85. In 1993 and 1994, he "only" ran the last 7 miles—starting at his statue. He was Grand Marshall in 1995. He did not run then and has not run since.

He ran his first Boston Marathon in 1928 but did not finish—one of only 3 he left uncompleted out of 61. He first watched it in 1921. He did not finish a Boston Marathon until his third try in 1933. He won his first in 1935 and his second in 1945. He finished second seven times and among the top ten finishers nine other times. He was an Olympian three times and won many national titles. He was the first road runner ever inducted into the National Track and Field Hall of Fame. Officials waived the retirement stipulation of five years before induction because they feared he would never retire.

➤Continue on Commonwealth 2.35 miles to Chestnut Hill.

Heartbreak Hill is perhaps the most famous section of the Boston Marathon. Mile 20.7 in Newton Hills, just past the *Young at Heart* statue, marks Heartbreak Hill's beginning. It climbs for the next 600 meters. It is the last of Newton's hills and is not particularly steep or long. It lies near the race's end. The largest number of marathon dropouts quit in Newton, perhaps dismayed by Newton's hills and attracted by the nearby Woodland T Stop. Despite its name's obvious aptness, it was not so named because of it. When Johnny "the Elder" Kelley overtook Ellison "Tarzan" Brown in the Newton Hills during the 1936 Boston Marathon, Kelley tapped Brown's shoulder in passing as a rival's friendly, playful gesture. The tap spurred Brown to greater efforts. He went on to win, repassing Kelley on the final Newton hill and, as a *Boston Globe* reporter wrote, "thereby breaking Kelley's Heart."

➤ Pass the gates of Boston College.

Here runners can first see the John Hancock Building, their landmark guide to the finish line.

A Jesuit college, Boston College's McMullen Museum of Art has strength in Gothic and Baroque tapestries, sixteenth- and seventeenth-century oil paintings, nineteenth- and early-twentieth-century American landscape paintings, and Japanese prints. Its Burns rare book and Bapst art libraries are also of interest.

➤ Enter Boston College T Stop, Green Line.

Walk 14B

Boston Marathon:
Downtown/Back Bay, Boston

General location: Boston's Back Bay.

Special attractions: A great elevated view of Boston and visits to Boston Marathon statues, monuments, memorabilia, and finish lines in delightful Back Bay.

Difficulty rating: Easy; flat on good sidewalks with protected crossings.

Distance: 0.8 mile.

Estimated time: 30 minutes.

Services: Restrooms and water are available at Prudential Center. Food and drink are available throughout.

Restrictions: None.

Downtown Walk/Back Bay, Boston

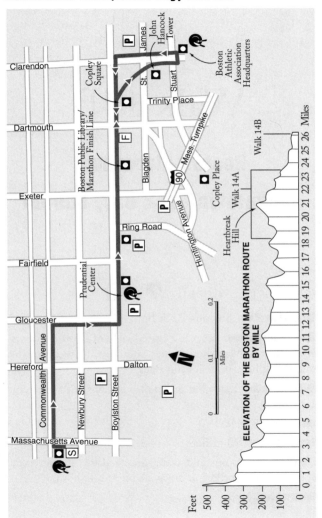

For more information: Contact Boston Athletic Association.

Getting started: Start at Eliot Hotel at Massachusetts and Commonwealth Avenues. Drivers access this walk from I-90 by exit 21, otherwise from I-93/Central Artery by exit 26 onto Storrow Drive and then left onto Massachusetts Avenue south. Covered commercial parking (wheelchair accessible, clearance 6 feet) is available by turning left onto Boylston Street to Prudential Center on your right as marked. Pedestrian garage access is from Boylston. Reach the start 0.35 mile away by turning left on Boylston across Massachusetts and then right to the corner of Commonwealth.

Public transportation: Go to Hynes/ICA T Stop and end at Copley T Stop, Green Line. Reach the start 0.25 mile away by turning left on Boylston across Massachusetts, then going right to the corner of Commonwealth. MBTA bus routes 5, 9, 10, 39, and 55 stop at Prudential Center (see "Getting Started" to reach the start).

Overview: This walk, with its Boston Marathon landmarks and mementos, is for those interested in the marathon, but unable or unwilling to go to Newton for Walk 14A, or for those wishing to take both walks.

The first "marathon" was run in 490 B.C. A Greek soldier, Pheidippides, ran from the Marathon battlefield, where Greeks had just defeated an invading larger Persian army, to report victory to an Athens anxiously awaiting news. Defeat would have meant for the Greeks enslavement by the Persians. According to legend, Pheidippides ran 24.8 miles, then collapsed and died after first crying to the city fathers, "Rejoice, we are victorious." Greek marathons were run at the ancient Panhellenic Olympics. The marathon was an official event in the first modern Olympic Games in Athens in 1896 and has been run at each Olympics since. The modern marathon distance was established at London's 1908 Olympic Games. The royal family wanted to see both the start from Windsor Castle and the finish in front of the Olympic Stadium's Royal Box, following a stadium lap run. That distance was 26 miles, 385 yards—the official marathon distance ever since.

This walk takes you to the several historic finish lines of the Boston Marathon and by marathon memorabilia and monuments through the lovely streets of Back Bay.

The Walk

➤Start at Eliot Hotel on Massachusetts and Commonwealth.

The former bartender at the hotel's lounge induced every marathon winner for years to put his footprints into concrete in the sidewalk in front of the hotel and identified each with a brass marker. The Eliot Lounge, its bartender, and the brass markers are all gone, but you can still see the footprints in the cement. Clio in the hotel is a great, but expensive, dining spot.

Visible farther left on the horizon down Commonwealth is the Citgo sign mounted atop a building. Known to runners as "1 mile to go," it is approximately 1 mile from the finish line. At its base is Fenway Park. Each marathon, Red Sox fans leaving an afternoon exhibition game cheer the passing runners.

➤Turn right and stay right 0.2 mile to Gloucester Street.

➤Turn right and stay right 0.1 mile to and cross Boylston.

➤Turn left and stay right 0.05 mile to the front of Prudential Center.

Elizabeth and Katie Clarke, the authors' daughters, on the Hare (of The Hare and Tortoise*) statue, Copley Square, Boston's Back Bay.*

Of Interest

Categories of Marathon Runners

Originally all runners competed against each other. This excluded women contestants and barred all but the most able from meaningful competition. Today there are special runner categories. The change has occurred only recently, gradually, and in the face of much opposition.

A difference dividing competition in each category or division is gender, with purses or recognition given to both the fastest man and the fastest woman in each group. A woman first competed—unofficially—in 1966, officially—because she did not disclose her sex—in 1967, and openly in 1972.

Competition is within each category except for the Overall/Open Division, where each competitor vies for the largest purses. There are divisions by age. There is a Wheelchair Division—its first entrant competed in 1975. There is also competition for the visually impaired. Special bonus purses go to any marathon runner breaking a gender world or course record.

The bronze statue of the nude man reaching up is Donald De Lue's 1967 *Quest Eternal*, epitomizing the Boston Marathon.

➤Continue on Boylston 0.05 mile to the Back Bay Brewing Company at No. 755. This is the location of the Tommy Leonard (Eliot Lounge's former bartender) Room with its trove of marathon memorabilia. Ask at the bar for directions. This is also a good dining and drinking place.

➤Continue 0.1 mile to Exeter Street.

On Exeter, between the Lenox Hotel and the new wing of Boston Public Library, is the site of Boston

Of Interest

Looking Down on Boston

Get a new perspective! Try it from the top. Boston offers several. Both John Hancock Tower and Prudential Center have observation decks from which, for a fee, you can look down on Boston and off far distances. The Bay Tower's restaurant, open to the public for drinks or dining in the evening, is topped by a three-story plate glass view of Boston Harbor, which is breathtaking on a clear evening. Peters Hill in Arnold Arboretum is the highest natural point in Boston. Dorchester Heights commands Boston Harbor—which is why the British had to evacuate! Go see why. Climbing Bunker Hill Monument is exhausting, but the chance to look out its windows is worth it. In East Boston, the top of the Don Orione Madonna Queen of the Universe National Shrine across Boston Harbor offers a stunning view. The panorama from atop Marriott's Custom House is grand!

Marathon's second finish line. It was in use for decades and stood in front of what was the Boston Athletic Association's clubhouse where the new library wing now stands. About 0.15 mile farther along the line of Exeter at Copley Place Mall (a premier shopping venue) is the site of Irvington Oval and the original finish line before the marathon's length was made 26.2 miles in 1927.

➤Continue 0.15 mile on Boylston to Copley Square.

Spanning Boylston beside the library is the painted current marathon finish line. A block farther in Copley Square to your right are Nancy Schsn's two 1994 bronze statues of a tortoise and a hare—characters from an Aesop's fable in which the plodding tortoise won a race against the faster but less diligent hare—commemorating

Boston Marathon's centenary. Embedded in the sidewalk nearby is the Marathon Monument. It shows the route of the Boston Marathon and the winner of each year's race. Four surrounding bronze posts celebrate other marathon categories—wheelchairs, women, sight-impaired, and age-defined—and commemorate towns along the marathon's route.

➤Cross Copley Square to the John Hancock Tower at 200 Clarendon Street. It is the large glass-fronted building before you. You can see the length of the entire marathon route from its observation deck.

➤Leave John Hancock Tower onto Clarendon for 0.1 mile, turn right, and stay right to and cross Stuart Street.

➤Turn left and cross Clarendon.

At 131 Clarendon are both the Hard Rock Cafe—drink and food are available and it is a hit with teenagers and rock 'n' roll enthusiasts—and the headquarters, on the eighth floor, of the Boston Athletic Association, which administers the marathon. Take the elevator to the association's offices to obtain marathon information and to see marathon memorabilia.

➤This is the walk's end. Return to Prudential Center and go to Copley T Stop, Green Line, by exiting the building, turning right on Clarendon to Boylston, then turning left for a block to the T stop or almost four blocks to Prudential Center.

Walk 15

Ocean Walk/Nahant-Lynn-Swampscott

General location: Nahant, Lynn, and Swampscott, about 12 miles north of Boston.

Special attractions: Ocean, sand beaches, sea bathing, and pleasant late-nineteenth- and early-twentieth-century seaside homes and cottages.

Difficulty rating: Easy; flat terrain over excellent walkways.

Distance: 2 miles.

Estimated time: 1 hour.

Services: Restrooms and water are available at Halfway House and Ward Bathhouse (in season) and at some commercial establishments en route. Food and drink are avail-

Ocean Walk/Nahant-Lynn-Swampscott

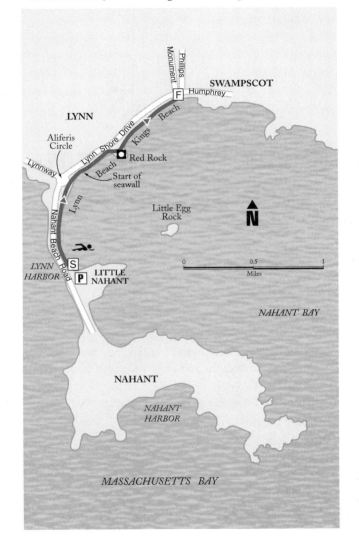

able (more in summer) en route, year-round in Swamp-scott.

Restrictions: Leashed dogs are permitted, but owners must remove dog waste and may not bring dogs on the beach between May 1 and September 30. Bicycles, horses, roller skaters, and pedestrians may not use the roadway—different from the walking path—on Lynn Shore Drive.

For more information: Contact the Metropolitan District Commission or the Park Headquarters (seasonal during the summer) at Ward Bathhouse.

Getting started: Start at Main Gate by the parking lot entrance off Nahant Beach Road on Nahant Neck where it joins Little Nahant Island. Drivers from Boston access this walk by U.S. Route 1 north to MA Route 129 and then east for 6 miles to the ocean, turn right and follow Lynn Shore Drive for about a mile to a traffic circle. Look for signs to Nahant and Nahant Beach Road, follow their directions and proceed about 0.8 mile, and then turn left at the end of the causeway to enter the uncovered parking lot (fee charged at peak season).

Public transportation: Commuter rail from Boston's North Station stops at Lynn not far from the beach. Follow Market Street east to Lynnway and continue north along the water for half a mile to the park. To return to the start from the end of the walk, take MBTA bus route 439 from Humphrey and Monument Avenue to the corner of Nahant Beach Road and Little Nahant Street.

Overview: You are on the Atlantic Ocean, so why not see it and walk along it? This is a particularly nice ocean walk, with great views of Boston in the distance and the charms, beaches, and nature reserve of Nahant and of historical Lynn Heritage Park nearby. The walking path is varied, from an asphalt path along dunes and beach grasses to a

A view along the walk with Boston's skyline in the background, Lynn.

broad concrete walk atop a seawall with steps permitting access to the beach and water. In season, the public beach has lifeguards and is open to sunbathers and swimmers.

The Walk

➤Start at the Main Gate and enter the car-free paved pathway. Turn left with Nahant Bay on your right and Nahant Beach Road on your left for 0.7 mile to the seawall walk.

Walk through an area of small sand dunes where wild roses, beach grasses, and similar sand beach–loving plants grow. There are no significant trees or structures on the neck. Picnic tables line the path. Lifeguards are here during the summer. About 0.8 mile down the path, near Aliferis Traffic Circle at the juncture of Nahant Beach Road and Lynn Shore Drive, is Halfway House with its toilet.

➤Turn right on the seawall walk and proceed for 1.3 miles to Phillips Street.

At the seawall walk, the path, the political entity, and the scenery all change. The path turns right, changes from asphalt to concrete, joins a seawall built along the ocean shore to prevent erosion, leaves Nahant, and enters Lynn. A shoreline drive replaces treeless sand dunes with vistas to either side. Handsome, architecturally interesting homes shaded by trees often look out on the path and the sea. At several points you may descend concrete stairs to walk along the sand beach. You will pass two points of land. The second—the result of a volcanic eruption half a billion years ago—is called Red Rock and is a great place to lie on the grass and enjoy the view.

From Red Rock, follow Kings Beach into Swampscott as Lynn Shore Drive becomes Humphrey Street.

There are benches along the path. This is a good place to stop and look back over the path, Nahant, Nahant Bay, and the Boston skyline. There are a number of places to eat at the end of the path along the beach in Swampscott.

➤Stop at Phillips Street. Take MBTA bus route 439 from adjacent Monument Avenue's intersection with Humphrey to Nahant Beach Road on Little Nahant Island or walk back to the start.

Walk 16
Salem

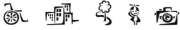

General location: Salem center, 16 miles northeast of Boston.

Special attractions: The Peabody Essex Museum, the old waterfront, handsome nineteenth-century residential buildings, and sites associated with Nathaniel Hawthorne and the witch trials.

Difficulty rating: Easy; flat terrain over good sidewalks.

Distance: 1.2 miles.

Estimated time: 1 hour.

Services: Restrooms and water are available at museums, the Visitor Center, and the Salem Maritime National Historic Site. Food and drink are available throughout.

Restrictions: None.

For more information: Contact the National Park Service Regional Visitor Center.

Salem

SALEM HARBOR

House of Seven Gables

Maritime Site

Derby Wharf

Central Wharf

Turner

Hardy

Bentley

Daniels Street

Derby Street

Orange

Hodges

Herbert

Union

Congress

Pleasant Street

Winter Street

Salem Common

Washington St.

Hawthorne

New Liberty Street

Visitor Center

Museum Neighborhood Center

Peabody Essex Museum

Howard

Brown

Essex Street Mall

Lafayette

Charter Street

Old Burying Point Cemetery

Marketplace

Washington Street

Essex

North Street

Summer Street

Cambridge

Chestnut

Pickering

Flint

0   0.1   0.2

Miles

N

Getting started: Start at Flint and Chestnut Streets. Drivers access this walk from Boston via U.S. Route 1 north to MA Route 16 east to MA Route 107 north and right onto Chestnut to Flint. Park on the street. Unless retracing your route on foot or using the Salem Trolley, take MBTA bus route 451 from Derby at Hawthorne to Salem Station and then the 450 to Essex and Flint Streets near the start.

Public transportation: From Boston's North Station, take commuter rail to Salem Station. Walk 5 minutes to the Visitor Center. MBTA bus routes 450, 455, and 459 leave from Boston's Haymarket for Salem. There is a Harbor Express Salem Ferry running a route from Logan Airport to Boston's Long Wharf to Salem Harbor as well as an A.C. Cruise Lines boat stopping at Salem Harbor on a route from Boston's 290 Northern Avenue Pier to Gloucester. The Salem Trolley runs a route touching Salem's tourist sites.

Overview: Salem has history, the sea and the Salem Maritime National Historic Site, beautiful architecture, a great museum (the Peabody Essex), and the chill of witchcraft. Come be bewitched!

Salem was settled by Puritan Roger Conant in 1626. Its generally poor harbor was, unlike most major East Coast ports, not the mouth of a major river. Salem was Massachusetts Bay Colony's capital from 1629–1630. By 1790, it was a prosperous shipping center engaged in trade worldwide, America's sixth largest town, and the richest American community per capita. Salem's ships' customs duties paid for almost a tenth of America's national budget between Independence and the War of 1812. Many of its fine homes are from this period. After the War of 1812, Salem quickly lost its preeminence to other ports and, consequently, its wealth. Salem's most famous

Nathaniel Hawthorne Statue, Salem.

son is Nathaniel Hawthorne, who was born (1804), lived, and worked here. He wrote *The Scarlet Letter* and *The House of Seven Gables,* among other literary works.

The Walk

➤Start on Chestnut's northeast corner with Flint, staying left 0.2 mile to Cambridge Street.

Chestnut is arguably America's finest concentrated collection of Federal-style architecture. Neighboring streets are nearly as fine. The Stephen Phillips Memorial Trust House (built in Danvers in 1800 and moved to Salem and enlarged in 1821) at No. 34 is open to the public and has authentic early American and English furnishings and other items. Hamilton Hall (1805) at No. 9, named for Alexander Hamilton, is open to the public weekdays.

➤Turn left on Cambridge and stay left a block across Essex Street.

➤Turn right and stay left 0.4 mile to and cross New Liberty Street.

The 1768 Ropes Mansion and Gardens at 318 Essex—part of the Peabody Essex Museum, open irregularly to the public—contains eighteenth- and nineteenth-century furniture and collections of porcelain and Irish glass.

The 1642 Witch House at 310 1/2 Essex is among America's oldest houses and the home of Judge Jonathan Corwin. Period-dressed guides dispense information about the period and the witch trials.

On your right across the street at New Liberty is the Peabody Essex Museum. A visit here is a must! This museum is only part of a larger complex of nearby sites under the same administration, including the Phillips Library

Salem's Witch Trials

Salem was not alone in its witch trials and executions. Boston had them. Europe executed more witches in the period than did Salem. Nonetheless, to Salem goes the fame because great literature and drama, principally Arthur Miller's play, *The Crucible*, chose it as a setting. The actual witch hysteria took place in Salem Village—now called Danvers—a couple of miles away.

Judge Jonathan Corwin presided over pretrial hearings of accused witches and examined the bodies of suspected witches for "Satan's marks" at his home in Salem. The site of the original dungeon that held the witches is at 4 Federal Street.

The existence of witches was accepted in 1692. The biblical injunction that a witch not be suffered to live was taken as an obligation. An epidemic of hysteria—or cynical manipulation—by a group of teenage girls capitalized on this belief and led to irresponsible charges of witchcraft by them against an ever widening circle of people. When the charges reached too high into society, the episode was brought to a close.

About 160 individuals were accused. Many fled prosecution. Of those who were tried, only one was found not guilty. That person was retried, found guilty, and hanged. Of 21 hanged as witches, 13 were women, 6 were men, and 2 were dogs. One man was pressed to death with heavy stones. All those executed denied being witches. The constable who arrested the first group later said he thought the girls were lying. He was hanged. Others died in confinement. Some confessing to witchcraft were spared.

It began in late January. By late November the witch hysteria was over. Chastened Salem declared public mourning and repentance. Many of the victims' heirs were paid compensation.

Salem today commercializes—heavily—its witch trial connection.

and 11 period houses. Begun in 1799 by Salem sea captains who wanted a place to display things they brought back from Asian voyages, it was originally the East India Marine Society. It is the oldest U.S. museum and has grown into a magnificent collection. It has six distinctly different collections—Early American Architecture and American Decorative Arts, Asian Export Art, Natural History, Asian, Oceanic, and African—as well as more than 400,000 objects and 3 million books, manuscripts, and works of art on paper. It fills two city blocks and several off-campus sites and has more than 30 galleries, a major research library—the Phillips—28 historic properties, 4 period gardens, 2 museum shops, and a cafe. An adjacent Oriental Garden is worth a visit.

➤Turn left on New Liberty and stay right a block to Brown Street.

The National Park Service Regional Visitor Center is at 2 New Liberty and features exhibits on early settlement, the maritime age, leather and textile industries, and a 27-minute multimedia film about the history and development of Essex County.

➤Turn right on Brown and stay right a block to Washington Square, which encircles the handsome Salem Common.

➤Circle Salem Common clockwise for 0.7 mile, keeping left, to Hawthorne Boulevard at Essex.

Surrounding Salem Common are some uncommonly attractive Federal-style houses from the turn of the nineteenth century by Samuel McIntire, Salem's preeminent architect. See particularly the houses at 74, 82, and 92 Washington Square East.

Across Essex is Bela L. Pratt's 1925 bronze statue of Nathaniel Hawthorne—an author who principally wrote about early Boston/Salem themes and a native of Salem. His first wife, Sophia Amelia Peabody, was among the first recognized American women painters.

➤ Turn right on Essex and stay right a block to and cross New Liberty.

To your right is the Peabody Essex Museum Neighborhood with its Phillips Library and relocated period buildings.

➤ Turn left onto New Liberty and stay right two blocks to and cross Derby Street.

At the corner with Derby is the Old Burying Point Cemetery and its associated Salem Witch Trial Memorial. Both are of interest for witch trial and other historical reasons.

➤ Turn left and stay right 0.3 mile to the entrances—on your right and left—to the National Maritime Site.

The street and Derby Wharf are both named for Elias Hasket Derby of Salem, America's first millionaire.

➤ Turn right and walk 50 feet to the Orientation Center.

The Salem Maritime National Historic Site at 174 Derby Street preserves wharves and buildings of the Port of Salem from the seventeenth, eighteenth, and nineteenth centuries—including the 1820 customs house where Nathaniel Hawthorne worked—on its 9.2-acre scenic waterfront. Here is the mooring for the *Friendship*, a

171 foot-long reproduction of the square-rigger *Friend-ship,* an East Indian merchant ship from the Great Age of Sail. It sails and is used as an educational vessel.

➤Return to Derby, turn right, and stay right 0.15 mile to the walkway just past Hardy Street.

➤Turn right and stay right 50 feet to the House of Seven Gables.

The House of Seven Gables Historic Site has the 1668 mansion made famous by Hawthorne's novel and includes Hawthorne's birthplace, three dwellings from the seventeenth century, seaside gardens, and a cafe.

➤Retrace your route to the start or take MBTA buses to Essex and Flint or the Salem Trolley to the Stephen Phillips Memorial Trust House near the start.

Walk 17

Walden Pond/ Concord-Lincoln

General location: Approximately 20 miles northwest of Boston and 1.5 miles southeast of Concord.

Special attractions: Walden Pond, Thoreau's original cabin site, a Thoreau cabin replica, and nature walks.

Difficulty rating: Easy; well-maintained trails over generally level terrain.

Distance: 1.75 miles.

Estimated time: 50 minutes.

Services: Wheelchair-accessible restrooms are at parking lots near Reservation Headquarters, Main Entrance. Wheelchair-inaccessible restrooms are available in summer at the Main Beach Bathhouse. Picnicking (no formal

Walden Pond/Concord-Lincoln

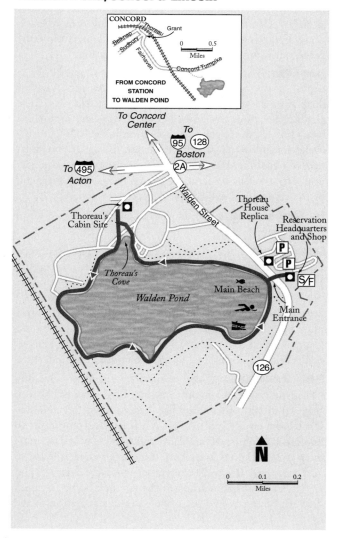

picnic areas), fishing, and swimming (in summer on Main Beach with a lifeguard) are permitted. There are boat launches. Guided tours are offered with advance reservations. Food and drink are seasonally available from concessionaires in the Main Entrance parking lots.

Restrictions: The reservation opens at 5 A.M. and closes at 8 P.M. in the summer and opens at 7 A.M and closes at dusk after the end of daylight savings time. No pets, fires, alcohol, flotation devices, motorized vehicles, motorized boats (except those using electric motors), camping, or bicycles are allowed, and the trash you bring in you must take out again. Do not disturb plants, animals, or the natural setting of the reservation. When the parking lot is full or the reservation overcrowded, access is restricted.

For more information: Contact Walden Pond Reservation Headquarters.

Getting started: Start at the Walden Pond Headquarters. Drivers access this walk from the south and east by taking I-95 (those coming from the north may join I-95 by taking I-93 or U.S. Route 3 south) to exit 29 onto MA Route 2 west and turning left (and those coming from the west may take MA Route 2 east and turning right) onto Walden Road (MA Route 126) and going to the uncovered Walden parking lots (a fee is charged) on the left.

Public transportation: Take commuter rail from Boston's North Station to Concord Station. Turn left on Thoreau Street and stay left to Belknap Street. Turn left and stay left to and cross Grant Street. Turn left and stay right to and cross Sudbury Road. Turn right and stay left as Sudbury swings right. Continue left along Fairhaven Road to and cross MA Route 2 (Concord Turnpike). Turn left and stay right to a path marked to the site of Thoreau's cabin. Turn right and follow the path into the reservation to the

A replica of Thoreau's Walden Pond cabin, Concord.

Literary Boston/Cambridge/Concord

Boston was early a leading literate center. America's first printer was located in Cambridge, and its first Bible was published there. Boston had America's first public school and free public library. Harvard was America's first college. Puritan clerics were published scholars. Phylis Wheatley, an eighteenth-century slave in Boston, was a published and widely read poet who George Washington asked to meet, and met, when he led the Patriot Army in Boston.

There were two principal centers of literary activity near mid-nineteenth-century Boston. One was Concord, centered on Ralph Waldo Emerson. Emerson (1803–1882) graduated from Harvard, was—but chose to cease to be—a Unitarian minister, developed the philosophy of Transcendentalism, and lived and wrote first from his family's Concord home, the Manse, and then from Emerson House in Concord. Around him gathered Nathaniel Hawthorne, Henry David Thoreau, Louisa May Alcott, and others. The other was Cambridge, centered on Harvard University. Prominent among Cambridge literati was Henry Wadsworth Longfellow. Both groups revolved around Boston, principally at meetings of the Saturday Club and at their publishers, Ticknor and Fields, in what is now the Old Corner Bookstore. The two groups and their Boston successors, such as Henry James, dominated American letters for most of the nineteenth century. They helped make Boston the nation's principal center for publishing and established such an aura of authority that non-Bostonian writers were compelled to come and seek their approval—or to publicly complain of their arrogant assumption of the role of national literary arbiter. *The Atlantic Monthly* magazine, long America's authoritative determiner of taste and literacy, was founded in and published from Boston.

John Marquand, Harriet Beecher Stowe, and the philosopher/poet Kahlil Gibran are just a few other literary names associated with Boston. Boston is still a city of intellectual discourse, publishing, and authors.

cabin site and pick up the walk at that point.

Overview: Henry David Thoreau and his Walden Pond stay are famous. See Walden Pond and Thoreau's cabin site and cabin replica as you enjoy a hike by the water among trees and utilize the reservation's many recreational opportunities.

Walden Pond is a 62-acre, deep, clear "kettle" pond formed by melting glacier ice set on a 400-acre reservation. It is open to the public year-round during scheduled hours and is operated by the Massachusetts Office of Environmental Management. The "Ice King" Frederic Tudor, a global commercial ice magnate of the 1840s, harvested ice from the pond and sent it—packed in insulating sawdust—by clipper ship to be sold in the tropics of Asia.

Henry David Thoreau—pronounced "THOR-oh"—(1817–1862) was a Harvard graduate from a prosperous family and close friends with Ralph Waldo Emerson from his hometown of Concord. He experimented with self-reliance by sleeping in a one-room cabin he built on Walden Pond for two years, two months, and two days during 1845–1847 in accordance with Emerson's Transcendentalist ideas. He was not isolated at Walden Pond, only a couple of miles from Concord. Friends and admirers regularly visited him at his cabin, and he frequently went to Concord to socialize and sell his vegetables and wild game. His contemporaneous notes of his stay were published in 1847 as *Walden,* a book that would make him famous in his own time and idolized by some even today. Nearby are the Concord Museum, with a Thoreau Gallery including Thoreau memorabilia, and the Thoreau Institute—visitors and researchers are only admitted with advance permission—with much information about Thoreau, his time on Walden Pond, and his thoughts and written work. Thoreau's birthplace and gravesite may be visited in Concord.

The Walk

➤Start at Reservation Headquarters, a place for supplies or information. Visit Thoreau's cabin replica near the entrance to the Walden Street parking lots.

➤Cross Walden Street and enter the reservation.

➤Continue along the path for 100 feet toward the pond (clearly visible) to the Pond Path.

➤Turn right. Go past Main Beach, Red Cross Beach, and Thoreau's Cove 0.45 mile to a paved path leading to the right on the far side of Thoreau's Cove.

➤Turn right and walk 0.1 mile to the marked original Thoreau cabin site. Thoreau was a firm advocate of individual personal liberties and of the abolition of slavery. He spent a single night in jail for refusing to pay a poll tax and described this martyrdom for principle in his work, *Civil Disobedience*. You may add to a stone cairn begun to Thoreau's memory in 1872.

➤Retrace your path for 0.1 mile to the Pond Path.

➤Turn right and continue along the pond's perimeter past Ice Fort Cove, Long Cove, Little Cove, and Deep Cove to Main Beach for 1.1 miles to the park entrance path.

➤Turn right and retrace your steps to the start.

Walk 18

Minute Man Trail/Lexington-Lincoln-Concord

General location: Between Lexington and Concord approximately 20 miles northwest of Boston.

Special attractions: A walk among woods and fields in a historical setting with displays and presentations at the Minute Man Visitor Center and Hartwell Tavern.

Difficulty rating: Easy but lengthy; flat gravel paths and boardwalks.

Distance: 5 miles one way.

Minute Man Trail/Lexington-Lincoln-Concord

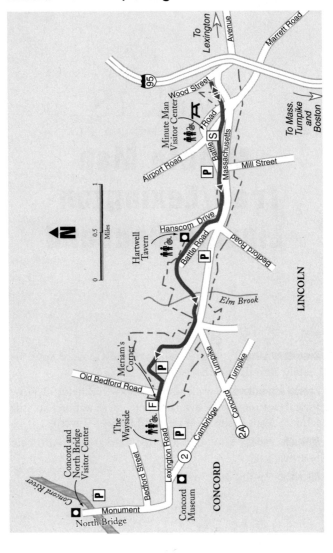

Estimated time: 2.5 hours one way. This is a linear walk. To return to the start, you must walk, take a taxi, or use two automobiles—one at either end. A public transportation solution is planned. Check with the park office.

Services: Restrooms and water are available at the Minute Man Visitor Center, near the Hartwell Tavern, and near Meriam's Corner. Except in winter, you will find fruit stands along Route 2A. Food and drink are available in and near Concord and Lexington. Picnicking areas are available at the Minute Man Visitor Center and near the Hartwell Tavern. There are special programs and historical reenactments. Rangers regularly lead walks, and ranger-guides are often present at the Visitor Center and the Hartwell Tavern.

Restrictions: Parts of Battle Road are not park-owned and carry heavy traffic. Private families live in the park. Their privacy must be respected. Metal detectors may not be used. Nothing may be disturbed in or taken from the park. Remain on designated trails and off farmers' fields and farm roads. Park only in designated parking lots. Leashed dogs are allowed. No horses or motorized vehicles are permitted. Seasonal cross-country skiing is permitted.

For more information: Contact Minute Man National Historical Park.

Getting started: Start at the Visitor Center. Drivers access this walk from the south and east by taking I-95 (those from the north may join I-95 by taking I-93 or U.S. Route 3 south) to exit 30 (and those from the west may take MA Route 2 east to the Concord Turnpike Cutoff) onto Lexington/Massachusetts Road west (except those coming from the west, who go east), which connects Concord and Lexington between which towns the walk lies. Free uncovered parking lots are along the trail. Park at the easternmost lot and follow signage 50 feet to the Visitor Center.

Public transportation: Take commuter rail from Boston's North Station to Concord Station or MBTA bus routes 62 and 76 from Alewife T Stop, Red Line, to Marrett Road and Massachusetts.

Overview: The battles of Lexington and Concord began the American Revolution. See where much of the action happened, visit restored colonial-era buildings, cross boardwalks over marshy wildlife sanctuaries, all while strolling through lovely New England countryside.

Americans had died earlier by British bullets, but on April 19, 1775, both first fired on and killed the other. There were 73 British dead, 174 injured, and 23 missing, while 49 Americans died, 40 were wounded, and 5 missing. War between them continued until one bested the other eight years later. Seven hundred British troops left occupied Boston by ship the day before. Their delayed departure permitted the Americans to organize and gather. Earlier that day, Redcoats at Lexington Common killed 8 of the 77 militiamen gathered there. This was more an error than a battle. The British marched for Concord, looking for stored arms and munitions and the leaders Samuel Adams and John Hancock. Minute Men advanced on British positions at North Bridge. The Redcoats obeyed the order to open fire, and the Patriots responded with the same. British withdrawing to Boston drew their flankers into the mass of troops when crossing the bridge at Meriam's Corner at the western end of this walk. The Americans fired into the British column from nearby hidden positions. Thereafter, until they returned to Boston, the British received constant sniper fire. The land was then open, unwooded fields. Most American fire was ineffective because long range, but it was devastating when terrain permitted the Patriots to come near. The British leadership was incompetent, and the Redcoats were near panic until able General Lord Percy's arrival. His 1,000 reinforcements and cannon prevented a British military disaster.

The Walk

➤Start at the Visitor Center.

Orient yourself regarding what lies along the trail and its significance before you begin your walk. Rangers can answer your questions. There are interpretive exhibits; a 40- by 15-foot mural of the fighting along the Battle Road on April 19, 1775; life-sized display figures of Joseph Hosmer, Lieutenant Frederick Mackenzie, and other important figures; a film presentation entitled *To Keep Our Liberty;* a book shop; and a multimedia program entitled *Road to Revolution,* providing an audio-visual time line of the events of April 19, 1775. Parts of the park not covered in this walk are in Concord: "The Wayside" house with its literary connections and North Bridge, where the "shot was fired heard round the world."

Longer than elsewhere in America, Massachusetts had known greater autonomy and profited more by evading British laws that would have stifled trade and industry. Consequently, British reassertion of control, imposed taxes, restrictive trade and shipping laws, and other harsh measures were most resented in and around Boston. Bostonians were the leaders in raising American displeasure to the level of armed revolt against British colonial rule. James Otis early denounced the Writs of Assistance. Paul Revere was both practical activist and propagandist. Samuel Adams was rabble-rousing orator, wily organizer, and thoughtful promoter of independence. This led to the Redcoats' march on Lexington and Concord.

➤From the Visitor Center, take the trail left 0.25 mile toward Lexington to a fork.

After crossing Airport Road at the Bluff, you leave the Battle Road—which British troops followed from their first engagement in Lexington to the Battle of Concord and along which they returned under murderous fire from Patriot militiamen firing from concealed positions.

➤Take the left fork 0.5 mile to the end of the trail.

On your right near the end is the marked Ebenezer Fiske House site.

➤Turn around and take the path for 0.5 mile, keeping left at the fork near the leg's start to the Bluff.

Fiske Hill—the scene of fighting at close quarters when British flankers tried to flush out Patriot snipers on the hillside—is marked on your right.

➤Retrace your path 0.25 mile to the start.

➤Continue down the trail 1 mile to a trail fork.

As marked, the Thomas Nelson, Jr., House site is on your right and the Josiah Nelson House site is farther on your right. After the trail takes a sharp right turn, you leave Battle Road. As marked, you come to the Paul Revere capture site where Revere was captured—and later released—by British soldiers. His companion rider from Boston, William Dawes, was turned back. Samuel Prescott—who had fortuitously joined Revere along his ride when they met as Prescott returned from an evening's amorous adventure—fled to reach Concord and successfully warned the Patriots there of the approaching British.

Minute Man Statue, Lexington.

➤At the fork, take the trail to the right 0.5 mile to Hartwell Tavern.

You will pass the 1693 William Smith House (open to the public) on your right. Smith, the captain of the Lincoln militiamen, and his wife, Catherine, lived here. You soon thereafter rejoin Battle Road. After passing the marked Samuel Hartwell House site on your right, you will come to Hartwell Tavern.

Open to the public, Hartwell Tavern (1733 with later additions) was the home of Ephraim and Elizabeth Hartwell and their children and was also a prosperous farm and typical tavern of the time. Costumed historical interpreters perform traditional crafts and answer questions about themselves and their times. The tavern is furnished with period items, including eighteenth-century children's toys. You will find antique breeds of farm animals in the barnyard, and historical reenactors are often in encampment near the tavern.

➤Return to the trail, turn right, and continue 0.25 mile to Bloody Angle, the site of an ambush staged by the Patriots, which caught the British soldiers in a crossfire and resulted in eight British dead, among the highest British casualty rates during their withdrawal under fire to Boston. From here you are no longer on Battle Road but are on a path.

➤Continue 1.5 miles to Meriam's Corner.

You will twice use boardwalks to cross swampy land. These are good nature observation areas. Pass, as marked, Job Brooks House on your left, past fields first farmed in the seventeenth century and the route for approaching militiamen on the day of the battle on your right, and past the Meriam House—from the late seventeenth century and one of the oldest houses in Concord—on your right.

The Meriam House and barn gave cover to militiamen who approached the British column marching back from Concord across the bridge at Meriam's Corner. It was here the first shots were fired that began the running battle on the remaining 16 miles of road back to Boston.

➤Continue 0.25 mile to the end of the trail and return to the start by foot or other means.

Walk 19

Garden in the Woods/Framingham

General location: About 5 miles north of Framingham Center and 20 miles west of Boston.

Special attractions: Wildflowers in a natural setting.

Difficulty rating: Moderate; gravel paths on rolling hills.

Distance: 1 mile.

Estimated time: 30 minutes.

Services: Restrooms, water, and a written guide listing nearby dining places are available at the Visitor Center and Education Building. Soft drinks and snacks are sold at, and a picnicking area is near, the Visitor Center. The route is safe, but bring insect repellent and be careful of

Garden in the Woods/Framingham

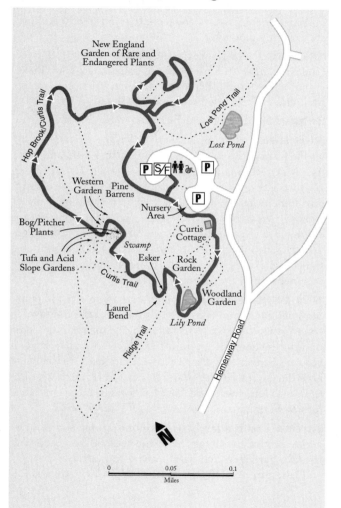

New England Garden of Rare and Endangered Plants

Lost Pond Trail

Lost Pond

Hop Brook/Curtis Trail

Western Garden

Pine Barrens

Nursery Area

Bog/Pitcher Plants

Curtis Cottage

Tufa and Acid Slope Gardens

Swamp

Esker

Rock Garden

Curtis Trail

Woodland Garden

Laurel Bend

Lily Pond

Ridge Trail

Hemenway Road

N

0   0.05   0.1
Miles

footing. There are benches along the trail, and research facilities are open to visitors. A bulletin board displays full information—including color photographs—of wildflowers currently blooming.

Restrictions: There is a fee. No pets or smoking are allowed. Children under 16 must be accompanied by adults. Picking of flowers or other environmental disturbances are prohibited. The garden is closed in winter.

For more information: Contact Garden in the Woods.

Getting started: Start at the marked Visitor Center clearly visible from parking lots. From the north, south, and east, take MA 128 to U.S. Route 20 west, go 8 miles on Route 20, turn left on Raymond Road, go 1.3 miles, turn right on Hemenway Road, and look right for entrance signs. From the west, take I-90 to exit 12, then MA Route 9 east 2.4 miles to the Edgell Road exit, turn left onto Edgell, go 2.1 miles, turn right onto Hemenway, and look left for entrance signs. Free uncovered parking is available near the entrance. Go to the Visitor Center.

Public transportation: Take commuter rail to Framingham Station (about 5 miles away), move toward the train's rear, cross Concord Street (MA Route 126), turn left and stay right to the boarding point for LIFT buses 2 and 3 across Howard Street. Take Bus 2 (leaves every hour on the half-hour during the day) to Water Street and Hemenway, turn right on Hemenway, and look left for entrance signs. Return to Framingham Station by LIFT bus 2 or 3.

Overview: This is a lovely walk among woods and flowers whose attractions change with the seasons. It is a special treat for gardeners and wildflower enthusiasts.

Dating from 1932 (the work of Will C. Curtis, a land-

A watery garden scene, Garden in the Woods, Framingham.

Other Boston Area Gardens of Note

Walks in this book passing near or through, in part or in whole, notable gardens include Walk 1 (Public Garden), Walk 8 (the Fenway Rose Garden, the Japanese garden at the Museum of Fine Arts, and the interior garden at the Gardner Museum), Walk 10 (Arnold Arboretum), Walk 13 (the Ware Glass Botanical Collection in Harvard's Natural History Museum), Walk 16 (the traditional and Japanese gardens of the Peabody Essex Museum), and this walk. Walk 1 evokes thoughts of the "Hidden Gardens of Beacon Hill" show each May while Walk 12 brings to mind the Horticultural Society's annual spring flower show.

Mount Auburn Cemetery in Cambridge is effectively a large and lovely garden, as is Forest Hills Cemetery in Jamaica Plain. Franklin Park in Jamaica Plain has its own renowned rose garden.

Farther afield but worth a visit is the Wooster Horticultural Society's Tower Hill Botanical Garden in West Boylston. In its initial stage of development is the Elmbank Garden in Wellesley being created by the Massachusetts Horticultural Society.

scape designer, and Richard [Howard] Stiles), the garden was given to the New England Wild Flower Society in 1965. It covers 45 acres of glacially sculpted terrain. All plants are labeled. Trails meander over wooded rolling hills, ponds, bogs, and streams past vistas of wildflowers, ferns, shrubs, and trees. A self-guided tour booklet is available and guided walks are offered. The garden is a living museum of temperate North American flora, but gardeners do remove unwanted varieties, trim trees, rake the autumn leaves, and apply fertilizer. It displays more than

1,600 varieties of plants, including over 200 rare and endangered species. Specially designed gardens showcase particular ecological environments and types of wildflowers. From early spring through late fall, the garden offers a continually changing variety of foliage and flowers. In late April, woods are filled with Virginia bluebells, bloodroot, and rare Oconee bells. By mid-May, hundreds of varieties of wildflowers are in full bloom, including blue wood phlox, yellow lady's-slippers, and showy trilliums. With summer, the carnivorous pitcher plants and delicate Calopogon orchids—among other varieties—shine among multicolored fields. In autumn, blue gentians, purple asters, and a display of colorful foliage and berries are the stars. Every season offers its distinct charms. Each repeated visit offers something new.

The Walk

➤From the Visitor Center, after purchasing tickets and obtaining desired materials, go to the nearby marked Trail Entrance.

➤Turn left and follow the marked Curtis Trail for 0.15 mile past the Curtis Cottage and nursery area to your right, through the Woodland Garden, and past the Rock Garden to your right, then circle to the left around Lily Pond.

➤Continue to the left 0.1 mile to the esker that divides the First from the Second Garden.

➤At the fork with Ridge Trail, turn and stay right 0.4 mile past Laurel Bend, through the Tufa and Acid Slope Rock Gardens and the swamp, left past the pitcher plants and the bog, through the pine barrens and Western Garden, and along the marked Curtis Trail/Hop Brook Trail.

➤Follow the path to your left leading (as marked) to the New England Garden of Rare and Endangered Plants and the Lost Pond Trail.

➤After 20 feet, turn and stay left for 0.1 mile along a short double-loop trail to see the New England Garden of Rare and Endangered Plants. Then turn left and circle and stay right for 0.15 mile along the larger loop from which you had diverted and rejoin your earlier path back to the main trail.

➤Turn left. Follow the Curtis Trail for 0.15 mile to the Trail Entrance.

➤Turn left and go to the Visitor Center where you started.

Appendix A: Other Sights

Greater Boston offers an almost infinite array of attractions. Those listed below are just a sampling of the many to be enjoyed in the Boston area. Not all involve walking, but each has delighted millions of tourists and residents. Have a great time.

Greater Boston

Walks in Progress

(617) 542-7696/(617) 367-6200/(617) 727-9547

A future great walk now exists only in parts. It is being developed by Boston Natural Areas Fund, the Trust for Public Land, and the Metropolitan District Commission. When completed, it will cross East Boston for 3.5 miles and include Wood Island Marsh, Belle Isle Marsh, and Constitution Beach. By ferry, it connects with a trail, sometimes referred to as the "Sapphire Necklace," along Boston's waterfront/downtown capitalizing on the new greenway where the Central Artery was. That joins parklands on either side of the Charles and, with a greenway connection to the Fens, links the walk to the Emerald Necklace. It also follows Boston Harbor to South End's Castle Island and from there 16 miles farther past beaches and the mouth of the Neponset River where the path divides. A shore leg runs a loop into the Squantum Peninsula and along the shore to Quincy. A 6-mile inland leg goes up the Neponset River and ultimately empties into Fowl Meadow Reservation and from there into 6,500-acre Blue Hills Reservation. A proposed 100-mile Bay Circuit Trail would start at Plum Island in Newburyport and run through Boston to Duxbury.

In Boston

Boston Harbor Islands State Park

Boston Harbor

(617) 727-7676; www.nps.gov/boha

Boston Harbor has more than 30 islands—some of them actually in Massachusetts Bay. They range in size from less than an acre to 214 acres and total 1,200 land acres scattered over 50 square miles of water. No other American city has so many islands so near. Some islands are joined to the mainland by landfill and causeways. Public ferries from Boston's Long Wharf, Hingham's Hewitt's Cove, and Lynn's Heritage State Park transport passengers to George's Island. From there, free water taxis go to Bumpkin, Deer, Gallops, Grape, Little Brewster, Lovells, Peddocks, and Thompson Islands. The islands are owned by both public and private interests. They were designated in 1996 as a National Recreation Area and made part of the National Park System. The various islands offer picnic areas, walking trails, camping, boating piers, swimming beaches with lifeguards, wildlife havens, food concessions, guided walks, historic buildings or ruins, and toilet facilities. Most islands are not accessible for the disabled, fresh water is not generally available, and camping facilities may be limited.

Castle Island

South Boston at the northeastern terminus of Norman J. Day Boulevard, Boston

(617) 268-5744

Castle Island is joined by fill with the mainland. Fortified continuously since 1634 by the renamed Fort Independence, it was rebuilt in 1854 as the fort you see today. It has not seen action since. Edgar Allen Poe served as a soldier in the fort and may have drawn on a dark, unfounded rumor as the basis for his story, "A Cask of Amontillado." Frederick Law Olmsted, the great landscape designer, is largely responsible for the appearance of the island and surrounding public beaches. Castle Island is administered by the National Park Service. Immediate to Castle Island are Pleasure Bay, a long waterfront promenade, fine public beaches, and fishing from Steel Pier. Get there by taking I-93/Central Artery exit 24 to Broadway Street's end, then left on Day Boulevard to its end, or by MBTA bus routes 3, 5, 7, 9, 10, or 11 to Broadway and Farrragut Avenue, walking the short distance to the beach, and then turning left and following the beach to Castle Island.

Franklin Park

Jamaica Plain, Boston
Zoo: (617) 635-7583/(617) 442-2002
Forest Hills Cemetery: (617) 524-0128
Samuel Adams Brewery: (617) 536-2739
This 520-acre park is part of Olmsted's Emerald Necklace. He considered it his best Boston achievement. It has been greatly changed since his day. Here are Boston's principal zoo (worth seeing), a fine rose garden, a public golf course (uninspired but cheap), and extensive untended heaths and woodlands. Nearby are Forest Park Cemetery—an interesting place to walk—and Samuel Adams Brewery, open for tours. Get there by taking Columbus Avenue (MA Route 28) west at any point from its start at Stuart and Arlington in Back Bay to the park. Public transportation is by MBTA bus routes 21 and 31 or Forest Hills (Orange Line) T Stop.

Outside Boston

Mount Auburn Cemetery

580 Mount Auburn Street, Cambridge
(617) 547-7105

Founded in 1831 by the Massachusetts Historical Society in imitation of Paris's Pére Lachaise cemetery that emphasized the natural beauty of the site and de-emphasized austere, funereal aspects, Mount Auburn Cemetery is 174 acres of great walks (10 miles of roads and paths), bird watching, gardens, and statuary. For horticulturalists, it is a "must see" on any Boston visit. It led a nationwide change in American cemeteries and became such a tourist attraction at the end of the nineteenth century that visitors had to be limited. Of the 87,000 people buried here (the number still grows), many have famous names. Some notables were even reburied here when the cemetery began, as a cachet to attract families of the lately bereaved! It is open daily 8 A.M. to 5 A.M. (7 A.M. to 5 A.M. during daylight savings time). A walking guide to the cemetery is available. Get there by taking MA Route 2 (Memorial Drive) west to Aberdeen and Mount Auburn Streets. By public transportation, take MBTA bus routes 71, 72, or 73 from Harvard Square T Stop.

Concord

(978) 369-3120

The town of Concord (about 20 miles northwest of Boston and near Lexington and Walks 17 and 18) is a lovely New England community with fine old homes, an interesting museum, some good dining spots, and natural beauty. It is also the site of much historical and literary interest. The first real battle of the American Revolution began here, and places related to it are well presented for the visitor. Concord's close association with major literary figures, such as Emerson and Thoreau, produced homes, graves, and other features pertaining to them. Get there by taking I-95 exit 29 and then going west on MA Route 2.

Public transportation (see Walk 17) to Concord is available by MBTA commuter rail.

Lexington

(781) 862-1703/(781) 862-1450

Near Concord and Walks 17 and 18 and about 12 miles northwest of Boston, Lexington played an important role in the first battle of the American Revolution. Although some of Lexington's Revolutionary sites and museums are interesting, its real charms lie in its buildings and other features that have survived from the eighteenth and nineteenth centuries. Several walks through town, guided by a Lexington Historical Society booklet, provide a pleasant day's outing. Get there by taking I-95 exit 30 and then going east on Massachusetts Avenue, or take MBTA bus routes 62 or 76.

Marblehead

(781) 631-2868

Marblehead, about 15 miles northeast of Boston and near Walks 15 and 16, is a charming and fashionable seaside community founded in 1629 with about 1,000 homes (many of sea captains) and buildings of the eighteenth and nineteenth centuries. It is a delightful place to be and dine in and has great walks by the sea, particularly over the causeway to Marblehead Neck. Get there from Boston by MA Route 1A (continuing as Lynnway), then left on Lynn Shore Drive/MA Route 129, or by MBTA bus routes 441, 442, 448, or 449.

Lowell

(978) 459-6150/(978) 978-5000

Lowell, about 25 miles northwest of Boston, was the site

of the beginning of America's industrial revolution and its modern textile industry in the 1830s. That history is showcased through the American Textile History Museum at 491 Dutton Street, the Lowell National Historical Park at 246 Market Street (the two above accessed off Lowell Connector at exit 5B), the Boott Cotton Mills Museum at 400 Foot of John Street, and the Working People Exhibit at 40 French Street. Get here by I-93 exit 44 and then I-495 west to a Lowell exit or from Boston by MBTA commuter rail.

Plymouth/Plimoth Plantation

Plymouth
(508) 747-7525/(800) 872-1620
Plymouth, about 30 miles southeast of Boston, was founded in 1620. The landing of the Pilgrims here—allegedly at Plymouth Rock—from the ship *The Mayflower*, on which they came from England, is a famous piece of national history. Descent from one of *The Mayflower*'s passengers is widely considered the mark of an elite American lineage. Plimoth Plantation at exit 4, MA Route 3, re-creates the Pilgrims' settlement of about 1627 and provides a living museum that emphasizes historical accuracy. There is also much to see and do in Plymouth itself, including a re-creation of the earlier boat, *The Mayflower II;* museums and monuments; and fine old buildings. There are walking trails and nature preserves in the immediate vicinity. Nearby cranberry fields are a colorful delight in early autumn. Get here from Boston by I-93/I-95/MA Route 128 and then south on MA Route 3 or by MBTA commuter rail.

Appendix B: Contact Information

Throughout this book, we have recommended that you contact the local attractions, museums, and visitor centers we mention to confirm opening times, locations, and entrance fees. The list below gives you the addresses and phone numbers (as well as websites, where available) for the places we have mentioned.

The Greater Boston Convention and Visitors Bureau has a wealth of information available about Greater Boston. Visit the visitor centers at the Common and Prudential Center, call the bureau's helpful staff, or visit their excellent website. "The Boston Globe Calendar," a Thursday weekly insert in a daily newspaper, provides current information on timely events. Also see the following websites: www.bostonmagazine.com, www.boston.com, www.mass-vacation.com, www.cambridge-usa.org, www.nps.gov/bost, and www.state.ma.us.

Greater Boston Convention and Visitors Bureau, (617) 536-4100/(888) 733-2678; www.bostonusa.com.

Boston Common Visitor Information Center, 147 Tremont Street, Boston; (617) 426-3115.

Prudential Visitor Center, Prudential Plaza, Boston; (617) 536-4100.

Attractions and Events

Boston Athenaeum, 10 1/2 Beacon, Boston; (617) 667-0270; www.boston athenaeum.org. Free, Monday–Friday, 9 A.M.–5:30 P.M.

Boston Public Library, Copley Square, Boston; (617) 536-5400.

Bunker Hill Monument/Pavilion, Charlestown, Boston; (617) 242-5641/242-7575.

Don Orione Madonna Queen of the Universe National Shrine, 111 Orient, East Boston, Boston; (617) 569-2100.

Emerson College Abbott Library, 150 Beacon, Back Bay, Boston; (617) 824-8500. Fine interiors.

Downtown Crossing, Boston; (617) 482-2139.

Ducklings Day Parade, (617) 426-1885.

Fenway Park, 4 Yawkey Way, Boston; (617) 236-6666; tours: (617) 267-1700; www.redsox.com.

Tours are conducted May–September, except on holidays or when there is a game before 5:05 P.M., on weekdays at 10 and 11 A.M. and at 12 and 1 P.M. (on non-game days, there is a 2 P.M. tour).

Fairsted, 99 Warren, Brookline; (617) 566-1689.

Faneuil Hall, Faneuil Hall Square, North End, Boston; (617) 338-2323.

Faneuil Hall Marketplace, Faneuil Square, North End, Boston; (617) 338-2323; events information: (617) 523-1300.

Fisher College, 118 Beacon, Boston, MA; (617) 236-8800. Fine interiors.

Goethe Institute, 170 Beacon Street, Back Bay, Boston; (617) 262-6050. Fine interiors.

Hamilton Hall, 9 Chestnut, Salem; (978) 744-0805.

Harborlights Festival, (617) 374-9000.

Hidden Gardens of Beacon Hill Tour, (617) 227-4392.

Hooper-Lee-Nichols House (Cambridge Historical Society), 159 Brattle, Cambridge; (617) 547-4252.

The House of Seven Gables, 54 Turner, Salem; (978) 744-0991; www.7gables.org. Entrance fee (under 6 free), open daily, 10 A.M.–4:30 P.M.

John Hancock Observatory, Copley Square, Back Bay, Boston; (617) 572-6429.

Longfellow House, 105 Brattle, Cambridge; (617) 876-4491.

Marriott's Custom House, 3 McKinley Square, Boston; (617) 310-6300.
Free historical tours at 4 P.M. daily. Peer into the inner workings of the tower's clock. View the harbor and city from the 26th-floor observation deck.

Massachusetts State House, 24 Beacon, Beacon Hill, Boston; (617) 727-3676.

New England Aquarium, Central Wharf, Boston; (617) 973-5266; www.neaq.com. Entrance fee (under 3 free; free to seniors), open Monday, noon–4:30 P.M., Monday–Friday, 9 A.M.–5 P.M., Saturday–Sunday, 9 A.M.–6 P.M.

Newton Free Library, 330 Homer, Newton; (617) 552-7145.

Nichols House, 55 Mount Vernon, Beacon Hill, Boston; (617) 227-6993.

Old Corner Bookstore, 1 School, Boston; (617) 523-6658.

Old State House (Bostonian Society), 206 Washington, Boston; (617) 720-3290; www.bostonhistory.org. Entrance fee, open daily, 9 A.M.–5 P.M.

Otis (Harrison Gray) House (Society for the Preservation of New England Antiquities), 141 Cambridge, Boston; (617) 227-3956. Entrance fee, open Wednesday-Sunday, 10 A.M.–5 P.M.

Phillips (Stephen) Memorial Trust House, 34 Chestnut, Salem; (978) 744-0440.

Prescott (William H.) House (National Society of Colonial Dames in Massachusetts), 55 Beacon Street,

Beacon Hill, Boston; (617) 742-3190.

Prudential Center Skywalk 50th-Floor Observation Deck, 800 Boylston, Back Bay, Boston; (617) 236-3318; www.prudentialcenter.com.

Revere (Paul) House, 19 North Square, North End, Boston; (617) 523-2338. Entrance fee (under 5 free), open daily, 9:30 A.M.–5:15 P.M.

Swan Boats, Public Garden, Boston; (617) 522-1966. From April 18 through September 20 (check for operating times, which vary from month to month). A fare is charged. Rides last about 15 minutes.

The Witch House, 310 1/2 Essex, Salem; (978) 744-0180.

Women's Educational and Industrial Union, 356 Boylston, Back Bay, Boston; (617) 536-5651.

Churches

Arlington Street Church, 351 Boylston, Back Bay, Boston; (617) 424-6625.

Church of the Covenant, 67 Newbury, Back Bay, Boston; (617) 266-7480.

Emmanuel Church, 15 Newbury, Back Bay, Boston; (617) 536-3355.

First Baptist Church Cambridge, 5 Magazine, Cambridge; (617) 354-3062.

First Church of Christ Scientist, 175 Huntington, Back Bay, Boston; (617) 450-3794; www.tfccs.com.

First Church Congregational, 11 Garden, Cambridge; (617) 547-2724.

King's Chapel, 58 Tremont, Boston; (617) 523-1749.

Old Cambridge Baptist Church, 1151 Massachusetts,

Cambridge; (617) 864-8068.

Old North Church, 193 Salem, North End, Boston; (617) 523-4848.

Park Street Church, 1 Park, Boston; (617) 523-3383.

Saint Paul's Cathedral, 138 Tremont, Boston; (617) 482-4826.

Tremont Temple Baptist Church, 88 Tremont, Boston; (617) 523-7320.

Trinity Church, 545 Boylston, Back Bay, Boston; (617) 536-0944.

Museums

Busch-Reisinger Museum, Otto Werner Hall, 32 Quincy, Cambridge; (617) 495-9400; www.artmuseums.harvard.edu. Entrance fee (fee also to Fogg and Sackler Museums; under 18 free/free to all Saturday mornings), open Monday–Saturday, 10 A.M.–5 P.M., Sunday, 1–5 P.M.

Children's Museum, 300 Congress, Museum Wharf, South Boston, Boston; (617) 426-6500, www.bostonkids.org. Entrance fee ($1, Friday, 5–9 P.M.), open daily, 10 A.M.–5 P.M., Friday, 10 A.M.–9 P.M.

Computer Museum, 300 Congress, Museum Wharf, South Boston, Boston; (617) 426-2800; www.tcm.org. Entrance fee (under 2 free), open daily 10 A.M.–6 P.M.

Concord Museum, 200 Lexington Road, Concord; (508) 369-9609, www.concordmuseum.org. Entrance fee, open Monday–Saturday, 9 A.M.–5 P.M., Sunday, noon–5 P.M.

Gardner (Isabella Stewart) Museum, 280 The Fenway, Boston; (617) 566-1401; www.boston.com/gardener. Entrance fee (under 18 always free; college students with IDs free on Wednesdays), open Tuesday–Sunday, 11:00 A.M.–5 P.M.

Gibson House Museum, 137 Beacon, Boston; (617) 267-6338.

Hart Nautical Gallery, 55 Massachusetts, Cambridge; (617) 253-5942.

Harvard University Museums of Cultural and Natural History, 26 Oxford/11 Divinity, Cambridge; (617) 495-3045; www.mcnh.harvard.edu. Entrance fee (free Saturdays 9 A.M.–12 noon), open Monday–Saturday, 10:00 A.M.–5 P.M., Sunday, 1–5 P.M. Do not miss the Ware Glass Botanical Collection!

Institute of Contemporary Art, 955 Boylston, Back Bay, Boston; (617) 266-5152.

Longyear Museum and Historical Society, 120 Seaver, Brookline; (617) 277-8943.

McMullen Museum of Art, Boston College, Newton; (617) 552-8100. Free, open summers: Monday–Friday, 10 A.M.–3 P.M.; academic year: Monday–Friday, 11 A.M.–4 P.M., Saturday–Sunday, noon–5 P.M.

MIT Museum, 265 Massachusetts, Cambridge; (617) 253-4444; web.mit.edu/museum. Free, open Tuesday–Friday, 10 A.M.–5 P.M., Saturday–Sunday, noon–5 P.M.

Museum of Afro-American History/African Meeting House/African-American National Historic Site, 8 Smith Court, Beacon Hill, Boston; (617) 742-1854; www.afroammuseum.org.

Museum of Fine Arts, 465 Huntington, Boston; (617) 267-9300; www.mfa.org. Entrance fee (17 and under free; Wednesday after 4 P.M., only a voluntary contribution), open Monday–Tuesday, 10 A.M.–4:45 P.M., Wednesday–Friday, 10 A.M.–9:45 P.M. (Thursday–

Friday after 5:00 P.M., only the West Wing is open), Saturday–Sunday, 10:00 A.M.–5:45 P.M.

Museum of Science, Science Park (Charles River Dam), Boston; (617) 723-2500; www.mos.org (also Mugar Omni Theater, [617] 523-2500, and Charles Hayden Planetarium, [617] 723-7500). Entrance fee, open Saturday–Thursday, 9 A.M.–5 P.M., Friday, 9 A.M.–9 P.M.

Old South Meeting House, 310 Washington, Boston; (617) 482-6439. Entrance fee (under 6 free), open daily, 9:30 A.M.–5 P.M.

Peabody Essex Museum, East India Square, Salem; (978) 745-9500/(800) 745-4054; www.pem.org. Entrance fee, open Monday–Saturday, 10 A.M.–5 P.M., Sunday, noon–5 P.M.

Sackler (Arthur M.) Museum, 485 Broadway, Cambridge; (617) 495-9400; www.artmuseums.harvard.edu. Entrance fee (fee also to Fogg and Busch-Reisinger Museums; under 18 free/free Saturday mornings), open Monday–Saturday, 10 A.M.–5 P.M., Sunday, 1–5 P.M.

Semitic Museum, 6 Divinity, Cambridge; (617) 495-4631; www.fas.harvard.edu/~semitic. Free, open Monday–Friday, 10 A.M.–4 P.M., Sunday, 1–4 P.M.

Tea Party Ship and Museum, Congress Street Bridge, Boston; (617) 338-1774.

***U.S.S. Constitution* Museum,** Charlestown Navy Yard, Charlestown, Boston; (617) 426-1812. Free, open daily, 9 A.M.–6 P.M.

Organizations

Ancient and Honorable Artillery Company, Faneuil Hall, Boston; (617) 635-7583.

Boston Athletic Association, 131 Clarendon, Boston; (617) 236-1652; www.bostonmarathon.org.

Boston Parks and Recreation, (617) 635-4505.

Harvard University, Cambridge; information and walking tours, (617) 495-1573.

Jimmy Fund Walk, Boston; (617) 632-3562.

Massachusetts Horticultural Society, 300 Massachusetts Avenue, Back Bay, Boston; (617) 536-9280; www.masshor.org.

Massachusetts Department of Environmental Management, (508) 866-2580/(800) 831-0569; parks information, (617) 727-3180.

Massachusetts Office of Travel and Tourism, (800) 447-MASS or (617) 727-3201.

Metropolitan District Commission, (617) 727-9547.

MIT Information Center, 77 Massachusetts Avenue, Cambridge; (617) 453-4795.

Thoreau Institute, Concord; (781) 259-4730.

Parks, Gardens, and Beaches

Arnold Arboretum, 125 Arborway, Jamaica Plain, Boston; (617) 524-1717. Free, open Monday–Friday, 9 A.M.–4 P.M., Saturday–Sunday, noon–4 P.M., closed holidays.

Boston National Historic Park, (617) 242-5644; www.nps.gov/bost.

Dorchester Heights National Historic Site, South Boston, Boston; (617) 242 9675.

Garden in the Woods/New England Wild Flower Society, Framingham; (508) 877-7630. Entrance fee (under 6 free), open daily, 9 A.M.–7 P.M. in May; daily 9 A.M.–5 P.M., April 15–30 and June 1-15; Tuesday–Sunday, 9 A.M.-5 P.M., June 16–October 31. Tours are given Tuesday–Saturday at 10

A.M. Last admission is an hour before closing. Closed November 1 through April 14. Many wildflowers purchasable April 15–October 31. Research facilities are open to visitors.

Jamaica Pond/Boathouse, Jamaica Plain, Boston; (617) 635-7396/635-4505.

Lynn-Nahant Beach Reservation, Lynn; (617) 727-1397 (seasonal).

Minute Man National Historic Park, 174 Liberty Street, Concord; (978) 369-6993/(978) 369-6993; www.nps.gov/mima

National Park Service Regional Visitor Center, 2 New Liberty Street, Salem; (978) 740-1650.

National Park Service Visitor Center, 15 State, Boston; (617) 242-5642

National Park Service Visitor Center, Charlestown Navy Yard, Charlestown, Boston; (617) 242-5601.

Salem Maritime National Historic Site, 174 Derby Street, Salem; (978) 740-1660.

Walden Pond State Reservation, 915 Walden Street, Concord; (978) 369-9609. Opens 5 A.M. and closes 8 P.M. in the summer and opens 7 A.M. and closes at dusk after the end of daylight savings time.

Theaters

Berklee Performance Center, 136 Massachusetts, Boston; (617) 747-8890; www.berkleebpc.com.

Boston Conservatory of Music, 8 Fenway, Boston; (617) 536-6340.

Colonial Theatre, 106 Boylston, Boston; (617) 426-9266.

Emerson Majestic Theatre, 219 Tremont, Boston; (617) 542-6772.

Loeb Drama Center/American Repertory Theatre, 64 Brattle, Cambridge; (617) 495-2668.

New England Conservatory of Music/Jordan Hall, 290 Huntington, Boston; (617) 536-2412; www.newenglandconservatory.edu.

Orpheum Theatre, Hamilton, Boston; (617) 679-0810.

Shubert Theatre, 265 Tremont, Boston; (617) 482-9393.

Symphony Hall, 301 Massachusetts, Back Bay, Boston; (617) 266-1492.

Wang Center/Music Hall, 270 Tremont, Boston; (617) 482-9393.

Wilbur Theatre, 246 Tremont, Boston; (617) 423-4008.

Transportation

A.C. Cruise Line, (800) 422-8419.

Airport Water Shuttle —Logan, Boston (Rowes Wharf), (617) 330-8680.

Amtrak, (617) 482-3660/(800) 392-6099.

Back Bay commuter rail, (617) 482-4400.

Bay State Cruise Company, (617) 748-1428.

Boston Harbor Cruises, (617) 227-4321.

Bradley Airport (Hartford/Springfield), www.bradleyairport.com.

City Water Taxi, (617) 422-0392 On-call water transportation between Logan Dock and more than ten Boston Harbor landings, April 1–October 15, 6 A.M.–8 P.M.

Greyhound Bus Terminal, 10 St. James Street, Boston; (617) 423-5810.

Harbor Express, (617) 376-8417; www.harborexpress. com (Salem, [978] 741-3442).

Logan Airport, www.massport.com/logan.

Manchester (N.H.) Aiport, www.flymanchester.com.

Massachusetts Bay Lines, (617) 542-8000.

Massachusetts Bay Transit Authority (MBTA), subways (Ts), commuter trains, and buses; (617) 722-3200 or 222-5000/(800) 392-6100; www.mbta.com.

Massachusetts Port Authority (MassPort), (617) 568-3100/428-2800; www.massport.com (call [800] 23-LOGAN, for questions regarding transportation to and from Logan Airport).

North Station commuter rail, (617) 227-5070.

Peter Pan Trailways (also for Bonanza Bus Lines and Plymouth & Brockton Street Railway Company), (800) 343-9999/(617) 720-4110.

Salem Trolley, (978) 744-5469.

South Station commuter rail, (617) 482-3660.

SmarTraveler, up-to-the-minute traffic information, (617) 374-1234; particularly valuable to avoid Big Dig snarls (also call [617] 973-5271 or see www.bigdig.com).

T. F. Green Airport (Providence, R.I.), www.tfgreen.com.

Appendix C: Great Tastes

Boston, the land of the bean and the cod, is home to Fanny Farmer, Julia Child, Joyce Chen, and some of America's hottest chefs. The diversity of the area's immigrants offers the world's cuisines. Boston provides a rare, and delicious, dining opportunity. Bostonians consume more ice cream annually than anywhere else in the country. Parker House rolls and Boston cream pie were created at Boston's Parker House Hotel. Porterhouse steaks got their name from Porter's Cattle Market Hotel in Cambridge. "Fig Newtons" were actually created in Cambridge. The name was chosen over "Fig Boston" and "Fig Sudbury" because it sounded better. "Scrod" is the white-fleshed fish most cheaply available on the docks that day. Hot dogs—as well as lobster and crab rolls—are served on a peculiar bun without an outside crust that is meant to be toasted before serving.

The following restaurants are far from the only, and not necessarily the best, in Boston, but they are good ones to try on the designated walks.

Anthony's Pier 4, 140 Northern Ave., South Boston, Boston; (617) 482-6262.
The sentimental favorite for seafood on the waterfront (Walk 5).

Back Bay Brewing Co., 755 Boylston, Back Bay, Boston; (617) 424-8300.
Fresh beer and Boston Marathon memorabilia (Walks 4/14B).

Bartley's Burger Cottage, 1246 Massachusetts, Cambridge; (617) 354-6559.
Great burgers with comic names, hilarious bohemian campus atmosphere (Walks 10/13).

The Bay Tower, 60 State, Boston; (617) 723-1666.

High prices but great views of Boston Harbor at night (Walks 3/6/14B).

Blacksmith House Pastry and Cafe, 6 Brattle, Cambridge; (617) 876-2726.

Site of Longfellow's blacksmith and his smithy (Walk 13).

Bull & Finch (*Cheers*), 84 Beacon, Beacon Hill, Boston; (617) 227-9605.

You saw it on TV, now be there in person—but expect to be in a crowd (Walks 1/2/4).

Cafe Louis, 234 Berkeley, Back Bay, Boston; (617) 266-4680.

Contemporary dining in a beautiful and historic Back Bay building (Walks 1/4/14B).

Chart House, 60 Long Wharf, Boston; (617) 227-1576.

Intimate dining in a historic building with an ocean view (Walk 5).

Clio, Eliot Hotel, 370 Commonwealth, Boston; (617) 267-1607.

Elegant dining with a marathon connection (Walks 4/10/14B).

Copley Plaza Hotel, 138 James, Back Bay, Boston; (617) 267-5300.

Gracious traditional dining on Copley Square (Walks 4/14B).

Curious Liquids Cafe, 22B Beacon, Boston; (617) 720-2836.

Drinks and snacks in Bulfinch's Amory-Ticknor House (Walks 1/2).

Durgin-Park, 340 Faneuil Hall Marketplace, Boston; (617) 227-2038.

Traditional New England dining—cheap, under spartan conditions, with trademark surly waitresses (Walks 3/6).

Figs, 67 Main, Charlestown, Boston; (617) 242-2229.
Gourmet dining in historic Charlestown (Walk 5).

Hampshire House, Library Grill, 84 Beacon, Beacon
Hill, Boston; (617) 227-9600.
In a grand old mansion above *Cheers* in every sense (Walks
1/2/4).

Harborside Hyatt Hotel, 101 Harborside Drive, East
Boston, Boston; (617) 568-1234.
Convenient dining on Harbor Walk (Walk 7).

Hard Rock Cafe, 131 Clarendon, Back Bay, Boston;
(617) 424-7625.
A franchised trendy favorite and a treat for teens and rock
music fans in Boston Athletic Association's building (Walks
4/14B).

Jacob Wirth Restaurant, 33–37 Stuart, corner Tremont,
Boston; (617) 338-8586.
Since 1868, a student bohemian atmosphere, great Ger-
man food, and at least 19 beers on tap (Walks 1/6).

Kelly's Roast Beef and Seafood, 10 Revere Beach Boulevard, Revere; (781) 284-9129.
Try the lobster rolls (Walk 7).

Lala Rokh, 97 Mount Vernon, Beacon Hill, Boston;
(617) 720-5511.
Handsome surroundings, classic Persian cuisine (Walks
1/2).

Legal Sea Foods at Prudential Center, 800 Boylston,
Back Bay, Boston; (617) 266-6800.
Great fresh seafood (Walks 1/4/5/14B).

The Locke-Ober, 3–4 Winter Place, Boston; (617) 542-
1340.
Since 1875, where Boston's stuffed shirts have stuffed
themselves (Walks 1/6).

Maison Robert, 45 School, Boston; (617) 227-3370.

Great French food in Old City Hall (Walk 6).

No-Name Restaurant, 15 1/2 Boston Fish Pier, South Boston, Boston; (617) 338-7539.

Cheap, great food (mostly fish) served on the pier in volume with indiscriminate seating at long picnic tables (Walk 5).

No. 9 Park, 9 Park, Boston; (617) 742-9991.

New, trendy restaurant in the historic Amory-Ticknor House (Walks 1/2).

Olives, 10 City Square, Charlestown, Boston; (617) 242-1999.

Renowned dining in historic Charlestown (Walk 5).

Parker's Restaurant, Omni Parker House, 60 School, Boston; (617) 227-8600.

A very "Boston" place to dine (Walks 1/2/6).

Rebecca's Bakery, 21 Charles, Boston; (617) 742-9747.

Light dining in the historic Charles Street Meeting House (Walks 1/2).

The Ritz-Carlton, 15 Arlington, Back Bay, Boston; main dining room, (617) 536-5700; lounge, (617) 536-5700.

Acclaimed food and beautiful rooms, overlooking the Public Garden (Walks 1/4/14B).

Santarpio Pizza, 111 Chelsea, East Boston, Boston; (617) 567-9871.

A favorite of many regular Logan Airport travelers (Walk 7).

Upstairs at the Pudding, 10 Holyoke, Cambridge; (617) 864-1933.

In the famous Hasty Pudding Club (Walks 11/13).

Warren Tavern, 2 Pleasant, Charlestown, Boston; (617) 241-8142.

Pub fare in a historic inn at moderate prices (Walk 5).

The Wayside Inn, 72 Wayside Inn Road off Route 20,

Sudbury; (978) 443-1776.

From 1706, the oldest operating U.S. inn and the eponymous setting for Longfellow's poem collection (Walk 19).

Ye Olde Union Oyster House, 41 Union, North End, Boston; (617) 227-1275.

America's oldest continuously operating restaurant, since 1826 (Walks 3/6).

Appendix D: Useful Phone Numbers

Police, Emergency, 911; Non-emergency, (617) 343-4200.

General Information and Referral, Greater Boston Chamber of Commerce, (617) 227-4500.

Hospitals, Massachusetts General Hospital, (617) 726-2000.

Newspapers, *Boston Globe,* 929-2000; *Boston Herald,* (617) 426-3000

Post Office, Rates and Information, (617) 654-5001/654-5223; www.usps.gov.

Public Library, Boston Public Library, General Information, (617) 536-5400.

Boston Road/Weather Conditions, (617) 228-4636/936-1234.

State Police, (617) 727-6780.

Appendix E: Read All About It

Bostonians and others love to read about and write about this city. Its writers are among America's greatest literary figures. The books below are only a few of those you will enjoy.

Nonfiction

Cleveland Amory. *Proper Bostonians*. Hyannis, MA: Parnassus Imprints, 1984. A great writer examines Boston society in 1917.

W. H. Bunting. *Portrait of a Port: Boston, 1852–1914*. Cambridge: Belknap Press, 1976.

Robert Campbell and Peter Vanderwerker. *Cityscapes of Boston*. Boston: Houghton Mifflin Co., 1992.

Monty Carlock. *A Guide to Public Art in Greater Boston from Newburyport to Plymouth* (revised edition). Boston: Harvard Common Press, 1993. Know the public art you see around Boston.

Michael Connelly. *26 Miles to Boston: The Boston Marathon Experience*. Hyannis, MA: Parnasus Imprints, 1998. For those with a special interest in the Boston Marathon.

Clinton Cox. *Undying Glory: The Story of the Massachusetts 54th Regiment*. New York: Scholastic Inc., 1991. The heroic story of the first black regiment in the Civil War.

George M. Cushing. *Great Buildings of Boston*. New York: Dover Publications, 1982.

Lawrence W. Kennedy. *Planning the City upon a Hill: Boston since 1630*. Amherst: University of Massachusetts Press, 1992.

Thomas H. O'Connor. *The Boston Irish: A Political History*. Boston: Back Bay Books, 1995.

Dan Shaughnessy. *At Fenway*. New York: Three Rivers

Press, 1996. For fans of the Red Sox and their stadium.

Louise Hall Tharp. *Mrs. Jack: A Biography of Isabella Stewart Gardner.* Boston: Little Brown & Co., 1965. A riveting read about a most interesting lady who was the scandal and delight of her Boston contemporaries.

Michael Tongias. *Exploring the Hidden Charles: A Guide to Outdoor Activities on Boston's Celebrated River.* Boston: Appalachian Mountain Club Books, 1997.

Walter Muir Whitehill. *Boston: A Topographical History* (second edition). Cambridge: Harvard University Press, 1968.

Cynthia Zaitzavsky. *Frederick Law Olmsted and the Boston Park System.* Cambridge: Belknap Press, 1982. A fascinating man and a great landscape designer, Olmsted played a critical role in making Boston's wonderful greenparks.

Literature

Henry James. *The Bostonians.* Kingston, RI: North Books, 2000. A masterly 1882 satirical view of Boston high society but in the context of a great psychological drama.

Nathaniel Hawthorne. *The Scarlet Letter.* Reading, PA: Addison-Wesley Educational Publishers, 1998. Salem's native son wrote about hypocrisy in puritanical early Boston in this 1850 book.

John P. Marquand. *The Late George Apley.* Cutchogue, MA: Buccaneer Books, 1994. Witty Pulitzer Prize–winning 1938 fictional insight into Boston's Brahmins in their final days of glory.

Robert McCloskey. *Make Way for Ducklings.* New York, N.Y.: Viking Press, 1941. Essential reading for children before visiting the Public Garden.

Edwin O'Connor. *The Last Hurrah.* Boston, MA. Little

Brown & Co., 1956. Fictionalized account of Irish machine politics in Boston clearly modeled after James Michael Curley.

Henry David Thoreau. *Walden*. Philadelphia: Running Press, 1990. Thoreau's classic 1854 account of his time on Walden Pond and his thoughts while there.

Appendix F: Local Walking Clubs and Tours

Boston has many organizations that regularly organize guided walks, some free, some for a fee, some for members only. Rangers (city, state, and national) lead tours around their parks. Some gardens and institutions offer special tours of their buildings and grounds. "The Boston Globe Calendar," a Thursday weekly newspaper insert, and other publications and websites publicize walking events.

Walking Clubs

There are two Boston-area Volkssport Clubs (American Volkssport Association, 1001 Pat Booker Road, Suite 101, Universal City, Texas 78148; [210] 659-2112/[800] 830-WALK/www.ava.org). They are Walk'n Mass Volkssport Club, www.ava.org/clubs/walknmass or Meltzwalk@aol.com; and Two Town Walking Club, jpiffat@aol.com.

Walking Tours

Boston Adventure Walking Tours, (617) 748-9569.

Boston by Design, (617) 232-9450.

Boston by Foot, (617) 367-2345/(617) 367-3766; www.bostonbyfoot.com.

Boston Center for Adult Education, (617) 267-4430.

Cambridge Center for Adult Education, (617) 267-4430.

Concord Museum, (978) 369-9763.

Discover Boston, (617) 742-1440.

Discovering Boston, (617) 323-2554.

Friends of Mount Auburn Cemetery Walks, (617) 547-7105.

Harvard University student-led campus tours, (617) 495-1573.

Haunted Footsteps Ghost Tour (Salem), (978) 745-0666.

Historic Neighborhoods Walking Tour, (617) 426-1885.

L'Arte di cucinare, culinary walks through the Italian North End or Chinatown, (617) 523-6032.

MIT guided campus tours, (617) 253-4795.

Ranger guided tours, Boston's Freedom Trail, (617) 242-5642/242-5689; Arnold Arboretum/Jamaica Pond, (617) 566-1689; Boston Park Rangers, (617) 635-7487; and Metropolitan District Commission Charles River Rangers, (617) 727-9659.

Society for the Preservation of New England Antiquities, (617) 227-3956, ext. 256.

Related Organizations

Bicycle Coalition of Massachusetts, (617) 491-7433.

Boston Duck Tours, (617) 723-DUCK.

Boston Sailing Center, Lewis Wharf, Boston; (617) 227-4198.

Community Sailing, Esplanade, Boston; (617) 523-1038).

Courageous Sailing Center, 1st Avenue, Charlestown, Boston; (617) 242-3821.

Hash House Harriers, Boston HHH, www.angelfire.com/ma/bostonhhh.

Piers Park Sailing Center, Piers Park, East Boston, Boston; (617) 561-6677.

Meet the Authors

Greg and Katherine Hawkins Letterman are enthusiastic urban walkers who reside in Kansas City, Missouri. Each has ties to, and a love for, Boston that has been acquired over decades.

Index